Flying
WITHOUT FEAR

DUANE BROWN, Ph.D.

New Harbinger Publications, Inc.

Publisher's Note

This publication is designed to provide accurate and authoritative information in regard to the subject matter covered. It is sold with the understanding that the publisher is not engaged in rendering psychological, financial, legal, or other professional services. If expert assistance or counseling is needed, the services of a competent professional should be sought.

Copyright © 1996 Duane Brown
New Harbinger Publications, Inc.
5674 Shattuck Avenue
Oakland, CA 94609

Cover design by SHELBY DESIGNS & ILLUSTRATES.
Text design by Tracy Marie Powell.

Distributed in the U.S.A. primarily by Publishers Group West; in Canada by Raincoast Books; in Great Britain by Airlift Book Company, Ltd.; in South Africa by Real Books, Ltd.; in Australia by Boobook; and in New Zealand by Tandem Press.

Library of Congress Catalog Card Number: 95-72224

ISBN 1-57224-042-3

First printing 1996, 4,000 copies.

To my wife Sandra who faced her fear of flying and
led the way for thousands of others.

Contents

Acknowledgments

I am indebted to many people for their contributions to this book. The people at the Federal Aviation Administration and National Transportation Safety Board warrant special praise because of their patience in providing answers to what must at times have seemed like trivial questions about the airline industry.

The pilots with whom I worked at American Airlines must also be singled out for thanks. Captain Bud Baldridge, Captain George Hazlehurst, Captain Jim Danahey, and Captain Dan Neufeld contributed to my knowledge and heightened the esteem with which I hold the people who fly the modern jetliners. If each reader could spend a few days with these pilots, you would be reassured that you really are in good hand when you fly.

Finally, another American Airlines pilot, Captain Steve Fryer, deserves special thanks, not only because he contributed to my knowledge as I worked with him in the now defunct American Airlines fearful flyer program, but because he took time to review Chapters 5 and 6 to make sure that the contents are accurate. No author can match the technical expertise of a professional pilot, and if there are any errors in those chapters, they are due to my interpretations, not Steve's knowledge.

1

Overcoming Your Fear
of Flying

The authors of a 1978 study sponsored by the Boeing Corporation estimated that twenty-five million Americans were afraid to fly at that time.
More recent estimates suggest that one in six adult Americans avoid airplanes altogether, which if correct, would mean that more than thirty-five
million people do not fly. The fact is that we are unsure how many people
fly while frightened, and what additional number avoid flying altogether.
I saw one study indicating that only about 6 percent of the people who
fly are totally comfortable. When groups of fearful flyers are given this
latter statistic they invariably respond, "Those that are totally comfortable
are the pilots."

Why are so many Americans afraid to fly? I believe it is partially
because of the continuous, often erroneous, message from the news media
that flying is unsafe. When there are reports about the safety of flying,
they are often interwoven with pictures or messages about crashes. It is
hard to assimilate information that flying is safer than driving when looking at the burned-out shell of an airplane in which several people were

killed. Furthermore, the media "loves" a plane crash. A plane crash provides interesting material that will fill pages or sound bytes for days on end. One telejournalist, who was himself a fearful flyer, reported that the people in his newsroom cheered when they learned that reporters in Sioux City, Iowa had a videotape of the 1989 United Airlines DC-10 crash that killed 111 people. That crash was featured in newscast after newscast all over the country, as are all spectacular crashes. Crashes that kill one or two people make the front page of the local newspaper.

Even airline incidents that should be non-events are highlighted. I turned on CNN's "Headline News" one morning to this headline, "Plane plunges 25,000 feet after depressurization." What really happened? The pressurization equipment on a USAir flight bound for Chicago failed. The yellow oxygen masks that deliver supplemental oxygen to passengers dropped out of their compartments, and the passengers placed them around their mouths and noses. The captain of the plane made what is termed an expedited (rapid) descent to 7,000 feet into airspace that had been cleared of other planes. The passengers took off their oxygen masks, and the plane proceeded to its destination. There was no plunge because the plane was in total control. Most of all there was no panic, something that many people who are afraid to fly fear almost as much as a crash. Many of the people who are afraid to fly are worried about the "quality" of their death on an airplane, fearing that they will know that death is inevitable for a long period of time before the crash takes their lives.

The fear of flying is not a uniquely American problem. Tens of millions of people from around the world are afraid to fly. In the American Airlines AAir Born seminars that I codesigned and conducted with my wife, Sandra, we had fearful flyers from Panama, Columbia, Mexico, El Salvador, Poland, Nationalist China, Chile, India, Russia, Finland, France, Canada, and England, and they all tell the same story: many of their friends are afraid to fly. The message here is simple. If you are afraid to fly, you are not alone.

The good news is that you can overcome your fear of flying if you are motivated, have at least a limited ability to trust other people, and are willing to spend a little time working on the problem. Motivation is the key. If you are trying to overcome the fear because your boss or spouse is pressuring you to do so, as opposed to wanting to rid yourself of a burdensome fear, you are likely to fail. Why? Because in your heart you believe that airplanes are unsafe. Moreover, you have probably been in arguments with the person or persons who are pressuring you, and to overcome your fear would be to admit that you are wrong and perhaps have been wrong for a long time.

Take a long look at your reasons for wanting to overcome your fear before proceeding. The fear of flying on most (not all) regularly scheduled airlines is an irrational fear. The first step toward flying without fear is to accept that it is irrational and that you want to put it behind you.

Fear of Flying: Its Costs and Benefits

If you are having trouble getting motivated, do a cost-benefit analysis of your fear; that is, make a list of the costs and benefits of being afraid to fly. Typically the costs far outweigh the benefits, although that is not always the case. I have known fearful flyers who lost their jobs because they would not fly, including one individual who lost a job that paid $200,000 a year. Others have turned down promotions, lost sweethearts and spouses, missed weddings and funerals and other family events, given away tickets to Hawaii and Paris, and turned down a ride on the Orient Express because of their fear.

More common costs involve the extra time and expense it takes to vacation in a Florida if you live in New England or to travel to Los Angeles for business if you live in San Francisco. It costs 30 cents per mile to operate the average automobile, which means that the cost of a round-trip from Los Angeles to San Francisco is about $330 plus meals. A one-way trip between the two cities takes from seven to eight hours if you have no problems. Round-trip airfare between Los Angeles and San Francisco costs less than $100, and the flight takes one hour each way.

One of the major costs of being afraid to fly that people overlook is the loss of self-esteem when irrational fears go unaddressed. I've had otherwise strong men and women break down and cry in my arms because they felt weak, strange, or on the verge of some catastrophic mental collapse because of their fear. I've never met a fearful flyer who felt better about herself or himself because they had the fear.

You can probably rattle off the costs of your fear, but the benefits may not be so easy to identify. One rather unassertive woman revealed that she had used her fear of flying to avoid traveling with her spouse. She decided to "keep" her fear because she really did not like her husband very much. A very assertive businessman revealed that if he got over his fear, he was going to have to share in a number of unpleasant assignments that his colleagues had allowed him to dodge because they knew he was afraid to fly. Others use their fear simply to control some of the events in their lives, such as vacations. Your fear may have more benefits than you realize. In your cost-benefit analysis, consider the following factors:

Costs	Benefits
Money lost	Money saved
Time lost	Time saved
Relationships damaged or lost	Relationships helped or saved
Self-esteem lost	Self-esteem gained
Other losses	Other gains

Trust and Motivation

The ability to trust others is also a key ingredient in overcoming the fear of flying. I have often asked people who are having difficulty letting go of the fear to rate their ability to trust others on a scale of one to ten, with one being almost completely unable to trust and ten being extremely trusting of other people. More often than not, the response is a one. One woman told me that the only person she trusted was her husband. Later she revealed that she kept secret savings and checking accounts. Clearly she did not trust her husband, or anyone else.

At this point I do not expect you to trust me or the contents of this book. As the book progresses I will try to earn your trust by displaying my expertise (I have helped hundreds of people overcome their fear of flying), my knowledge of the airline industry (I have studied it extensively), and the fact that I understand the pain that you suffer because of your fear and the impact it makes on your life (my wife was afraid to fly and did not do so for eight years). At this point, all I ask is that you have enough trust to stay with the book.

How much time will overcoming your fear take? The American Airlines AAir Born seminars lasted two days. Eighty-five percent of the people who enrolled in the seminars took the graduation flight on the second day. Of those who did not fly, about 5 percent continued to work on their problem and gained their ability to fly. The mental health professionals who operate the USAir, KLM, and FINNAIR programs report similar results, although most of these programs last a bit longer than two days. The amount of time it will take to overcome your fear of flying depends upon two factors already mentioned: trust and motivation. But it is a fear that can be conquered quickly if that is your goal.

Defining the Problem

On the surface, fear of flying seems like a simple matter, and for some people it is. However, it is important to understand the precise nature of your problem if you are to be successful in eliminating it.

Aviophobia

Some people are certain that if they fly, the plane will crash and they will die. These people suffer from *aviophobia* or, if you prefer, *areophobia*. In some instances these people will not fly at all. If they fly they may have intense anticipatory anxiety and nightmares about dying, although not necessarily in airplanes. During the flight, people who have aviophobia often listen intently to every sound, watch for other airplanes, scrutinize the flight attendants' faces for signs that something is amiss with the flight, sit very quietly so they will not disturb the equilibrium of the airplane, and pray or engage in superstitious rituals.

Claustrophobia

Other fearful flyers do not fly, or are uncomfortable on airplanes, because they are claustrophobic. Some airplanes, including almost all commuters as well as the McDonnell Douglas-built DC 9-80 and the Fokker 100, which is manufactured in the Netherlands, are quite small. The jet bridge to the plane, which can get quite crowded, can also present a barrier to people who are afraid they will be trapped in a small space and die.

The person who is truly claustrophobic is afraid of closed spaces other than airplanes and typically feels more comfortable in large planes than small ones. I say this because many people misdiagnose their problem with airplanes as claustrophobia because they have a feeling of not getting enough oxygen (choking) when they get frightened on an airplane. As you will come to understand, that feeling of not getting enough air is a common reaction for people who have any number of phobias, and for people who have anxiety attacks.

Acrophobia

A fear of heights, known as acrophobia, also keeps people off airplanes. Oddly, many people who suffer from acrophobia, including yours truly, are not afraid of flying at 35,000 feet. I know pilots who are afraid of heights! However, for some people, the *thought* of flying at 35,000 feet raises their anxiety, and being at that height results in waves of terror, particularly when the plane bounces or shakes as it often does in turbulence. Even when the plane is not shaking, people with acrophobia sit waiting for the inevitable fall. They envision the plane as suspended by a thread or sitting on a needle, either of which is about to be severed, with the result being that the plane will crash. Some acrophobics are not so much afraid that the plane will fall as they are that they will fall out of the plane. They view the flooring and the plane itself as fragile, and they believe that they will fall if they move about in the cabin.

A large group of people have combinations of these phobias. Many of the people I have encountered started with a single fear (for example, of closed spaces) and found that it spread to other things, such as tall buildings. Because this can occur, if you have a fear of flying, attack it vigorously now. It can spread, and contrary to popular belief, it often does not get better simply by flying repeatedly. It only gets better if you fly repeatedly and you cope with the fear.

Panic Attacks

Another large group of people who avoid air travel are not afraid of the plane crashing at all. These are the people who have panic attacks. People who have had panic attacks on planes tell me that they would have welcomed a crash to end the panic attack. For those of you who have never experienced a panic attack, it can best be described as losing control of your body. Your heart races (some people report that it feels as though your heart will literally jump out of your chest), your breathing becomes shallow, and you may become dizzy and disoriented. Many people who experience their first panic attacks go to the hospital emergency room thinking they are having a heart attack.

While it is important to note that the panic attack is *not* related to the environment in which it occurs (a panic attack in an airplane could just as easily have occurred in a department store), the person who has these attacks associates the attack with the environment and may begin to avoid those places and other similar places. Why? Partly because the driving urge when you are having a panic attack is to leave the place where it is occurring. Also, some people who suffer from panic attacks believe that they may die of a heart seizure because of their panic attack; or they may do something extremely foolish, such as take off all their clothes and run up the aisle; or they may end up with an incurable mental health problem. One fearful flyer, who was also afraid of buses, tunnels, and bridges, was certain that if he flew he would have a panic attack and end up in a catatonic state from which he would never emerge. Needless to say there is no place to go when you are flying several thousand feet above the earth, and it is that feeling of being trapped that activates the fear.

Fear of the Unknown

Finally, many people who have never flown are afraid to fly. In most instances they have developed a store of misinformation about airplanes, pilots, and the airline industry. Often their fear can simply be classified as a fear of the unknown. My experience with this group of people is that once they take the risk and fly, they love air travel.

Dealing with the Problem

It is often difficult to diagnose your own problem. When we asked people who came to our seminars to tell us the nature of their problem, they frequently could not do so accurately. This is particularly true of people who have, or have had panic attacks, because the thoughts and physical reactions to small spaces, heights, and airplanes are very similar. If you cannot determine the exact nature of your problem, proceed anyway. I will go into enough detail about the causes and symptoms of the fear of flying that it is likely that you will understand the nature of your problem before you reach the end. There are many commonalities in the treatment used, and this shotgun approach should be successful for you.

Aviophobics, claustrophobics, acrophobics, and people who have panic attacks have one common enemy: airplanes. However, they need somewhat different strategies for dealing with the problem. Aviophobics need reliable, trustworthy information, because they are walking sources of misinformation. The same is true of people who have never flown. Claustrophobics can benefit from information about the airplane and the industry, but what they need primarily is to understand the powerful hooks that underlie their fear and strategies for dealing with the fear. Acrophobics need information about the stability of airplanes, (such as how they perform in turbulence), as well as strategies for dealing with their fear on the airplane. Finally, there are bits and pieces of information about airplanes and the industry that will benefit flyers or would-be flyers who experience panic attacks; but what people in this group need is to develop the confidence that they can cope with their panic attacks.

What Will Be Covered

This book is divided into several sections based on the individual and collective needs of fearful flyers. In Chapter 2 I discuss how the fear develops and its impact on the way we think. A discussion of the physiology of fear follows in Chapter 3. Every fearful person needs to understand how fear affects the body and how to control the fear response. In this chapter the use of alcohol and drugs, strategies often adopted by the flying public, will be addressed.

Chapter 4 covers techniques for dealing with the cognitive and physical reactions to fears. Two chapters, 5 and 6, are devoted to providing objective facts about air travel. Over the last five years I compiled a list of the questions most often posed by fearful flyers. I then wrote answers to those questions and had those answers checked by a number of professional pilots. As a result I am completely confident that you are getting the best information available about flying and the airline industry.

In Chapter 7 I address one of the most debilitating aspects of the fear of flying—anticipatory anxiety. If you suffer from anticipatory anxiety, you must rid yourself of it to become a comfortable flyer. Chapter 8 takes you through a dress rehearsal for your first successful flight, and in Chapter 9 you will be asked to construct your own flight plan, a plan that you can use to maximize your comfort on airplanes. The final chapter, Chapter 10, makes a number of suggestions to help you maintain the momentum you gain when you fly successfully.

What Else Can You Do?

During your recovery from your fear of flying, there are several other things you can do.

Do not read or watch reports of air disasters. The reason for this is that, because you are afraid to fly, you have selective perception. What I mean by this is that you tend to focus on those things that *verify* your fear. I once held up a page of a newspaper emblazoned with captions that addressed two disasters. One story dealt with an air crash in Charlotte, North Carolina that killed thirty-eight people. The other story reported that thirty-one people were killed on Texas highways in one day. You can be sure that the fearful flyers focused on the air disaster, just as you search for details that justify your own beliefs.

Make every effort to visit airports during this period. Talk to pilots, flight attendants, and mechanics about their jobs and the industry.

However, do not ask flight attendants technical questions about flying. Save technical questions for the pilots and mechanics. As odd as it may seem, flight attendants get practically no orientation to issues such as aerodynamics, the air traffic control system, or airplane maintenance. The result is they know only slightly more about flying than the typical passenger and are a major source of misinformation about air travel. They may report, "We have been flying through storms all day" or "We hit an air pocket this morning." Both statements are laden with misinformation.

While you are visiting the airport, visit the control tower. This will give you some sense of how the air traffic control system works. In smaller airports you will need to arrange a tour by calling the airport manager's office. Larger airports may offer regular tours, but the place to start is still the airport manager's office.

Work on what I call contributory fears. If you are claustrophobic, construct a hierarchy of the closed spaces that scare you. Then, starting with the place that produces the least fear, begin to confront your fear by visiting these places. Similarly, if you are afraid of heights, begin to desensitize yourself by visiting places that produce the fear; again starting with those places that seem the safest. This process is outlined in Chapter 10, and if you are afraid of heights or closed spaces, you may wish to skip directly to the section in Chapter 10 that deals with these fears before you proceed.

If you are currently flying, do not schedule a flight that is likely to result in avoidance. By avoidance I mean that you do not board the airplane. If you schedule a flight, be 100 percent confident that you are going to get on the plane, even if you are going to have to "white knuckle" it. Avoidance increases the fear because of the tremendous sense of relief you feel when you fail to board the plane or simply cancel the flight. The emotion associated with anticipating the flight and then avoiding it heightens your memory of your fear as well. The result is that you will have a tendency to remember only the unpleasant aspects of flying. If you once flew comfortably, one of the signs of recovery will be that you begin to recover the pleasant memories associated with flying.

If you have panic attacks, practice coping strategies every day. Even if you have not had an attack for a long time, you must maintain the strategies you have developed for coping with them. Your fear is that you are going to have a panic attack, so you need to be prepared. Several strategies for coping with the thoughts and physical symptoms of panic attacks are outlined in this book, but I suggest that you purchase one of the books listed in Appendix B as well. Also, if you have become agoraphobic (afraid to venture far from home) and flying means leaving your safety zone, begin to push the boundaries of that zone in much the same way I describe in Chapter 10 people who have acrophobia or claustrophobia. A woman who had not left the safety of her neighborhood for several years told me to pass this word on to others like her: "All airports are pretty much the same and seem safe after you get used to one." If airports are not safe places for you at this time, visit your airport with someone you trust. Eat lunch (the food is likely to be bad though) and watch the planes take off and land.

Plan a celebration! Think about that place you have always wanted to visit and begin to make plans to *fly* there. Think of this trip as a reward for confronting this life-limiting fear. Airplanes and the ability to fly open up the world of leisure and business, the world of family and friends. As one of the pilots that I work with said, "They are better than a magic carpet. They take you to magical places and they provide restrooms and drinks." Your fear draws circles around you and keeps you from those magical places. It also keeps you from fulfilling your potential as a human being. It is time to put the magic back into your life.

Summary

The fear of flying is one of the most common fears in this country and throughout the world. It can be conquered in a relatively short period of time if you are motivated and are willing to spend the time acquiring valid information about flying and the airline industry. Take stock of your reasons for wanting to overcome the fear and try to identify your problem. Do you suffer from a phobia, such as claustrophobia; does the fear of a panic attack keep you from flying; or are you simply afraid of the unknown?

If you believe it is time to stop letting the fear of flying draw circles around your life, then proceed.

2

How the Fear of Flying Develops

Telling people how they develop the fear of flying is risky business, primarily because the types of problems people have are so diverse. After listening to hundreds of fearful flyers tell their stories, I have developed some insight into the sources of the problem. Researchers have also provided perspective on the development of phobias and panic attacks, which are the primary concerns of fearful flyers. In addition, some fearful flyers suffer from post-traumatic stress disorder, a problem that will be addressed briefly in this chapter.

Before discussing the development of the fear of flying, I want to reassure those of you who feel guilty about your problem that you have done nothing wrong. I urge you not to blame yourselves for being afraid to fly. Many fearful flyers curse themselves for being afraid of airplanes, closed spaces, or heights. When they have panic attacks they feel guilty, often for unspecified reasons, but the heart of their thinking is self-blame. Others get angry at their parents or spouses and blame them for the weakness they see in themselves.

By blaming yourself or others you actually reduce your ability to deal with your problem. It lowers your self-esteem, and you may alienate the people who could provide the support you need to cope with your fear. You need to be as strong as possible, and you need all the support you can get to overcome this or any other fear. Begin by accepting the fact that you have the problem and establishing the goal of ridding yourself of the fear.

At the outset I also want to point out that it is not necessary to know what causes your fear in order to overcome it. Since many people are curious about this, I include a discussion of the origins of the problem, beginning with the factors that predispose you to the development of simple phobias and panic attacks. The discussion ends with the impact these problems make on your thinking once they develop.

Heredity as a Predisposing Factor

Social scientists are increasingly convinced that heredity plays a significant role in the development of mental health problems and of normal personality traits as well. For example, it is possible to discern at an early age which children will be introverts and which will be extroverts. This suggests that the tendency to be more people-oriented is an inherited characteristic. It is not possible to tell which children will be afraid to fly, however. Ultimately, this fear develops as people interact with their environments, but the predisposition to develop the fear is probably hereditary.

How can you tell if you are predisposed to develop your fear? Look for the presence of irrational fears and panic attacks in your mother, father, siblings, aunts, uncles, and grandparents. If more than one-sixth of them have panic attacks or irrational fears, such as claustrophobia, acrophobia, or agoraphobia, you are probably disposed by heredity to develop one of these problems. Keep in mind that many people are predisposed by heredity to develop one of these problems and do not. Ultimately, most human behavior develops as a result of both heredity and environmental influences.

Childhood Environment as a Predisposing Factor

Certain childhood environments also play a role in the development of phobias and panic attacks. In some instances the relationship between these childhood environments and the development of the problem is obvious. For example, many people who develop phobias and panic disorders come from abusive homes. Children who have been sexually or physically abused by parents or relatives learn that they cannot trust people in their world, and this distrust generalizes to include the airline industry, pilots, and many others. Children who grow up with alcoholic parents or with parents who are addicted to other substances soon learn that their parents "love" the object of their addiction more than they love their children. These children also learn not to trust after being disappointed time after time by well-meaning parents who give in to their addictions rather than keep their promises to their children.

Some of the childhood environments that predispose children to develop irrational fears and panic attacks are not so obvious. Many of the hundreds of fearful flyers I have met over the years come from homes that appear to be idyllic in every way. Their parents love each other, and they and their families are free from financial worries. In fact many people who are afraid to fly come from affluent families. In these cases, one or both parents may overprotect the children. They forbid the children to take physical risks that their playmates are taking. For example, when other children get bicycles these children are told that bikes are risky and they can't have one until they are older. Parents also make decisions for the children that the children should be making for themselves. These decisions may range from little things, such as selecting clothes, to more important issues, such as choosing friends. Finally, because one or both of the parents are fearful, they worry about their children. Parents may go so far as to inculcate their children with the idea that the world is a scary place and they must be on guard at all times.

Overprotection can cause children to assume they are defective in some way. They see other children as more competent than they are. As adults, because they have been denied opportunities to take risks and make decisions, they may be less confident and have lower self-esteem. Parents who worry excessively may cause children to grow up with less ability to trust others and with the idea that there are many things to be afraid of in their environment. These children are also more likely to be worriers, a behavior they learned directly from their parents.

Some parents unintentionally teach their children not to trust people. In these homes children are told over and over again not to trust unless they have made absolutely certain that people are trustworthy. Since it is virtually impossible to verify the trustworthiness of many people, the adults who emerge from these homes trust very few people.

The common denominator for people who don't learn to trust themselves or others is "control." They want to control various aspects of their lives because it is the only way they can be sure of the outcome. It is this lack of trust, based on fear that manifests itself in numerous ways, including the fear of flying. Flying involves trusting a series of people you do not know and, in fact, cannot know. That is too big a leap of faith for people with a need to control events.

Finally, there are the parents who set impossibly high standards for their children and neglect to teach the children that perfectionism is an unattainable goal. As adults, these children are rarely satisfied with themselves. They are anxious about their own behavior because it does not attain a level they deem appropriate (perfectionism), and they distrust anything that they see as faulty. It is worth noting that not all perfectionistic people come from homes with parents who set high standards. One or more alcoholic parent can produce perfectionistic children. Some children in these homes feel that their parent's problem is partially their fault, and, if they are good enough (perfect), the problem will go away.

The Stress-Susceptible Personality

Not everyone who is genetically and environmentally predisposed to develop phobias and panic attacks actually develops them. However, they are likely to experience more stress because of their responses to other people and their views of themselves. As you probably noted in the section on childhood environments, many of them also influence their children, who have similar problems, trusting others. When people who have attended my seminars call and say they are experiencing trouble again, one of the questions I ask routinely is, "On a one-to-ten scale, with one being you almost always have trouble trusting other people, and ten being you trust almost everybody you know, how would you rate your ability to trust others?" The answers almost invariably are one or two.

In other instances, people who come out of what I have termed predisposing childhood environments do not trust themselves. They have low self-esteem, a lowered ability to take risks, and are perfectionistic in their thinking and actions. People who do not trust themselves or others are constantly engaged in safeguarding behavior. This manifests itself as the need to control the events and people in their lives, as mentioned in the previous section. Sometimes these people exert control through their jobs or positions and other times through manipulation and deceit. One fearful flyer confessed that she had convinced her spouse to go by car on every trip they had taken for twenty-five years so she could observe the beauties of nature. Other fearful flyers insist not only that they go by car, but that they drive. Another fearful flyer admitted, while she "trusted" her husband, she maintained secret bank accounts in the off chance their marriage should end.

People who cannot trust others or themselves lead stressful lives. If they cannot trust others, they must constantly be concerned about the nature of their relationships. If they have low self-esteem, they often expect to fail, even in the face of overwhelming success. If they are perfectionistic, regardless of their accomplishments, they feel they should have achieved at a higher level.

Traumatic Events

Post-traumatic stress disorder (PTSD) is usually associated with war veterans. However, many other people who have been involved in, or have witnessed, traumatic events develop this disorder. In some people the traumatic event may have occurred in childhood and the problem develops over time. In others the trauma occurred when they were adults and the disorder develops rather quickly. One fearful flyer saw her boyfriend killed in an automobile accident. Another fearful flyer was trapped for more than an hour in an automobile that had been hit broadside by a truck. A woman who developed PTSD after the death of her children, in addition to being afraid to fly, was afraid to go into tall buildings because she feared they would collapse. Many people who have been in severe earthquakes develop other fears, including the fear of flying. The result of the trauma is that individuals' belief systems are shattered.

Once again the concept of trust manifests itself. People who develop PTSD may not trust themselves, the people around them, machines or mechanical devices, or, as noted above, the integrity of physical objects such as buildings.

Stressful Life Experiences

Many people who are afraid to fly are puzzled by the development of the fear. They report having flown earlier in their lives with no trace of discomfort. If asked about the time period when the fear first developed, they often mention stressful life events, such as weddings, funerals, the birth of their first child, a promotion, or graduation from college or graduate school. At one time I told a standard story to seminar participants about the mythical newlywed who gladly boarded the airplane at the outset of the honeymoon, only to find that she was unable to board the plane to return home. I always finished this story with the line, "Must have been a great honeymoon," until one of the participants revealed that the story was exactly what had happened to her.

Rather than causing the development of phobias and panic attacks, stressful life experiences may act as triggers for these problems. In the case of the fear of flying, these stressful life events seem to stimulate people to think about their mortality. Some people begin to consider what would happen to others, usually their children, if they die. "Who would raise them?" "Would they have good parents?" "Would they have happy lives?" One woman confessed that she fixated on the fact that her husband might marry his secretary, a woman she characterized as a "bitch." Other people begin to consider what they would miss or lose if they died. "I'd miss being a doctor." "I'd miss seeing my children grow up." "I'd miss being the chief executive of my firm." Both types of thinking produce a heightened concern about death and the types of events that might produce it. Often, people who contemplate such things decide that airplanes are dangerous—a belief that had probably been instilled to some degree earlier in their lives.

Ironically, people who take alternate modes of transportation because they are afraid to fly are exposing themselves to a higher probability (statistically) of accidental death. As you begin to think about your fear, think of it as a deadly enemy that is trying to increase the probability you will die!

Catastrophic Thinking

Many people who develop phobias and panic attacks are worriers and catastrophic thinkers—they automatically assume the worst. My wife Sandra, who is a recovered fearful flyer, still has bouts of this style of thinking. On one occasion, I had to travel several hundred miles by car on business. Normally, before I start home, I call to give an estimate of my arrival time. This time, in my haste to get on the road, I neglected to call. When I arrived several hours later, Sandra had decided that I was dead of a heart attack along the highway somewhere, and she was preparing to call the state police to initiate a search for my body. I have never had a problem with my cardiovascular system!

Unfortunately, once the fear of flying develops, this type of thinking translates into automatic catastrophic thinking about airplanes. This thinking can be cued in dozens of ways, ranging from a frown on a flight attendant's face to an unusual noise coming from the hydraulic system that raises and lowers the landing gear.

Simple Phobias: The Role of Learning

Whether or not you are predisposed to be fearful, simple phobias, including the fear of flying, are learned, either through direct experience or vicariously. There are some exceptions for people who develop their fear of flying as a result of traumatic experiences. Even post-traumatic stress disorder is acquired through a powerful learning process that varies significantly from the processes described here. Direct learning experiences that lead to the fear of flying are of two types: those that involve danger and those that do not but are interpreted by the person to be dangerous. Vicarious learning is the process of acquiring information, skills, or habits by indirect means such as listening to or observing others, or by acquiring information through the media. Most fears, including the fear of flying, are acquired vicariously.

Direct Learning

A few people who develop the fear of flying have actually been in danger on an airplane. I have met and helped people who were in crashes and other types of accidents (remember, 60 percent of all people survive airplane crashes). However, most people who think they are in danger on an airplane are not. Let me give you several examples, and you tell me, are you in danger?

- The captain asks the flight attendants to be seated because of turbulent air ahead. Almost immediately the plane begins to resemble a mini-roller coaster.

- The oxygen masks drop out of their compartments because the air conditioning system fails.

- Smoke comes into the cabin and the captain announces that one engine is being shut down as a precautionary measure.

- Lightning strikes a plane.

The answer is no, you are not in danger in any of these situations. I'll explain why later in the book, but let's suppose that you thought you were in danger when one of these events occurred on one of your flights and no one set the record straight. You would get off the plane thinking that you almost lost your life; you were lucky to survive. Because you feel lucky to have survived, you do not want to get on another plane, but you do. On your next flight you expect that the event you experienced earlier will repeat itself and you will not be so lucky this time. Over time, your fear grows, and perhaps becomes unbearable. You might stop flying altogether or retreat into alcohol or pills to ease your fear.

The learning that occurs when you are actually in danger and when you think you are in danger but are not is the same: you become afraid to fly. If you have not developed a full-blown phobia, information will alleviate your fear; if you have, it will take all the strategies outlined in this book to overcome the fear.

Vicarious or Indirect Learning

As I stated earlier, most fears are acquired vicariously, either by word of mouth or through the media. Almost everybody has an opinion about airline safety. The next time you are at a party, wander around the room asking people if they believe airplanes are safe. Regardless of what they believe, ask them where they get their information. Few people, even those who think flying is safe, have a valid information base about flying.

The chances are quite good that you receive your word-of-mouth information from relatives, friends, and coworkers. Because you get your first information from your parents and relatives, if they are afraid to fly, the chances are good that you will be afraid to fly. If your parents provide you with invalid information about flying, the twin forces of heredity and environmental influences are working against you. When one parent is afraid to fly and the other is unafraid, the information from the one who is unafraid may offset the erroneous information that comes from the fearful parent.

The other basic source of information about flying for most people is the media. Journalists will tell you that what they report regarding emergencies is "the best available information at the time." Notice that they do not pretend that the information is factual, because they report opinions that often have little value. Let's take a look at a newspaper report that includes the best available information about a crash.

The Best Available Information?

The following are excerpts from the September 21, 1989 *New York Times* report of an accident at La Guardia airport.

> A USAir jetliner taking off for Charlotte, North Carolina from La Guardia Airport last night skidded off the end of a rain-slick runway and plunged into the bay near Rikers Island . . .

At the time of last night's crash, a National Weather Service meteorologist took a "special observation" of weather conditions at La Guardia, breaking with the routine of taking hourly weather readings at 10 minutes before each hour. Ralph Izzo, a Weather Service meteorologist, said he could not be certain whether the special reading was taken because of the crash or because of the perception that the area's weather pattern was shifting dramatically. . . .

While the plane [involved in the accident] has one of the longest and safest histories of any commercial jet, it has experienced some problems recently, particularly with its engines. But there was no initial indication last night that the plane that crashed had engine trouble.

The article goes on to report on accidents and incidents involving engine failures on the B-737-400, which was the type of plane involved in the accident.

By reading these excerpts, three potential conclusions could be drawn about the cause of the accident: a slick runway, rapidly shifting weather, and engine failure. The actual cause of the accident, according to the National Transportation Safety Board report, was that the plane's rudder was stuck in an incorrect position for takeoff, and the pilot delayed aborting the takeoff to the point that the plane could not be stopped on the runway.

Did the *New York Times* report the best available information? I don't think so. Obviously the reporters involved speculated about the potential causes and reported facts about the weather and the past mechanical problems of the type of plane involved based on their speculation. The result is that the typical fearful flyer interprets the information in the reports and concludes that the plane was flying under dangerous circumstances (slick runway, shifting weather, potentially faulty engines). Speculating about causes of crashes and cloaking that speculation in the guise of objective journalism, and reporting facts about accidents, are not the same.

More Examples from the Media

I have picked on the *New York Times* because it is one of the best U.S. newspapers, yet it engages in questionable reporting practices when airplane crashes are involved. In a September 9, 1994 article regarding a crash, reporter Richard Perez-Pena reported that the National Transportation Safety Board listed the probable cause of an accident involving a Fokker-built F-68 as icing, when in fact the probable cause was listed as pilot error. I could go on, but I won't. I will say that it is impossible for experts to make sense out of the typical newspaper report of an airplane accident because the reports are often unrelated to what happened.

Are television reports any better? No, because much of the news that is reported by telejournalists comes indirectly from wire services. As I noted in Chapter 1, CNN's "Headline News" reported that a plane plunged 25,000 feet after pressurization equipment failed. What really happened? The plane was flying at approximately 32,000 feet at the time the pressurization equipment failed. The oxygen masks dropped from their compartments, and the passengers placed them over their noses and mouths so they could breathe without difficulty. The captain requested immediate clearance from air traffic control to descend to 7,000 feet, and because of the circumstances, the clearance was granted. The plane descended rapidly, but under perfect control, to 7,000 feet. The passengers removed their oxygen masks and the plane flew safely to its destination. The word *plunged* used in this newscast means to move violently and rapidly downward and is a major distortion of what actually occurred.

Another type of major distortion that occurs in the news media has nothing to do with accuracy or the words used. It has to do with what is reported and how often it is highlighted. Some articles that highlight airline safety do appear in newspapers. One that I will describe in more detail in Chapter 5 reported on the world's safest airlines. However, articles featuring safety information are usually small and appear in the middle sections of the paper or at the end of television newscasts. On the other hand, news about major crashes appears on the front pages for days, and often contains information not only about the crash that has just occurred, but other crashes as well. The September 9, 1994 report of a crash in the Pittsburgh area in the *New York Times* contained several companion items, including a highlighted chronology of major crashes in the 1989–1994 period and an article that highlighted USAir's "shaky" financial status.

Because crashes are highlighted over and over again in newspapers and on television, safety information is underreported, data about past crashes is highlighted in stories about current crashes, and superfluous information is included in news stories, the flying public's view of flying is distorted. A twelve-year-old who had flown without fear all of her life watched the televised reports of the July 19, 1989 crash of a DC-10 in Sioux City, Iowa over and over. In August, when her family normally took their vacation, she refused to board the plane. She overcame her fear because the family took quick action, but her case illustrates how the media can contribute to the development of the fear of flying.

As I have noted throughout, not all people who are afraid to fly are actually afraid of the plane crashing. Some have other fears, such as claustrophobia (closed spaces) and acrophobia (heights). These fears develop in much the same way as aviophobia, although the media is undoubtedly less influential in the development of these fears. People who have panic attacks also avoid airplanes in many instances. In the next section, I deal with some specific factors that contribute to the development of panic attacks.

Panic Attacks

People who are afraid to fly often describe their reaction to their fearful thoughts as a panic attack. In fact, if you have ever seen or been the person who runs off an airplane because of the belief that the plane will crash or run out of air, you know that panic is the cause. The cue that initiates the response is the airplane. Panic attacks, sometimes called anxiety attacks, are not caused by the environment. They are the result of a combination of biological and psychological reactions that overstress the body. Panic attacks can begin early in a child's life, but they typically do not develop until after adolescence.

What is a panic attack? It is an involuntary physical response that has varying degrees of intensity. It usually involves shortness of breath (a choking sensation), muscle tension, a feeling of growing cold or warmth, and a driving thought to leave the situation in which the attack is occurring. In severe forms panic attacks can cause disorientation (not knowing where you are) and hyperventilation resulting in a temporary blackout.

Panic attacks can occur anywhere since they are not really brought on by the environment. However, once they occur, people who have them link them with the environment and begin to avoid the place where they occur, whether it is a supermarket, shopping mall, highway, bridge, tunnel, or airplane. Because the driving thought during a panic attack is to leave the situation in which it occurs, airplanes are one of the most feared environments. As one fearful flyer put it, there is nowhere to go at 35,000 feet.

What do people who have panic attacks fear? Sometimes it is death. During a panic attack the heart races, and some people who have them fear that they are going to have a heart attack. Others fear the intense discomfort they feel during the attack. Many people who have panic attacks are afraid that they will make a fool of themselves by passing out, screaming, or ripping off their clothes. A few people who have panic attacks on airplanes worry about attacking the flight attendants or breaking out the windows (which is impossible) in their attempts to escape.

Contributing Factors to Panic Attacks

As already mentioned, heredity and childhood environments contribute to the development of stress-susceptible personalities, which can increase the probability that panic attacks will occur. Entering stressful jobs and leading stressful lifestyles can also increase the likelihood of their development. People who abuse alcohol and drugs also are much more likely to develop panic attacks than other people, as are people who suffer from depression.

Dealing with Panic Attacks

Specific interventions are outlined throughout this book for people who have phobias and who suffer from panic attacks. However, the fearful flyer who has panic attacks needs to take a few additional steps. If you are an alcoholic, have a drug dependency, or are depressed, you need to seek treatment for these problems immediately. You should also get help from a qualified therapist for your panic disorder if you have not already done so.

You may need to make some lifestyle changes. Begin by eliminating caffeine from your diet. Caffeine increases heart rate and blood pressure and can increase the likelihood of your having a panic attack. The caffeine in two cups of coffee can increase your heart rate up to thirty beats a minute, and some soft drinks contain more caffeine than coffee does. Chocolate, tea, and some pain killers also contain caffeine. If possible, reduce the stress in your life, either by taking on less stressful assignments or enrolling in a stress management program. Even if you are not an alcoholic, avoid the use of alcohol before or during flying.

Finally, be careful to follow your normal exercise program before a flight. When you exercise, your body produces a substance known as sodium lactate. This substance, if present in amounts higher than the body's tolerance level, will often produce a panic attack in people who suffer from panic disorder. It is not unusual for people who are planning a flight to exercise more than usual, either because they are nervous or because they expect to miss exercise sessions during their trip. If you are subject to panic attacks, try some of the alternate relaxation techniques described in Chapter 4 for preflight jitters.

Automatic Catastrophic Thoughts

Whether you have a simple phobia or suffer from panic attacks, the thought of air travel may produce automatic thoughts of disastrous events. You can trigger these thoughts just by imagining being on an airplane, or they can be stimulated automatically by a plane passing overhead. You may also have dreams that deal with catastrophic flights, but just as likely they will be nightmares about death and dying or other unfortunate events. It is catastrophic thoughts that fuel your fear and produce the uncomfortable physical reactions you experience. It is also these thoughts that set you to worrying weeks and perhaps months before a flight and ruin your business trip or vacation once you have completed the first part of your trip.

You will learn that your beliefs—whether they are about airplanes or your reaction to the airplane—are based on erroneous information. At some point you will need to take a huge risk. You will have to believe that the information you now have is faulty and needs to be replaced. You will also have to acquire the skills to deal with your thoughts and your physical reactions. Chapter 3 is devoted entirely to helping you understand more fully what happens to you and how you can control the physical aspects of your fear. Later chapters will give you the techniques you need to conquer all aspects of your fear, including your catastrophic thoughts.

Once the Fear of Flying Develops

Once you develop an irrational belief, or for that matter any belief, you begin to process information selectively. You pay more attention to information that confirms or supports the established belief than information that discredits it. In straightforward terms, this means that if you believe that airplanes are unsafe or that they will fall out of the sky, you look for information to support that belief and you ignore or discount information that is counter to what you believe.

As I introduced myself to a group of fearful flyers in the Miami area, a young woman held up her hand and said, "I want you to know that I think American Airlines pays you to lie to us." I have often seen fearful flyers argue with airline captains who have twenty to thirty years of flying experience, claiming that their experiences or those reported in newspapers were more valid than the captain's knowledge and experience. Suspending your belief system about airplanes will be difficult, but it is essential to your recovery. I'll touch on this subject again at the beginning of Chapter 6.

Will the Fear Grow?

The answer to this question varies with individuals. I have met many former fearful flyers who conquered the fear on their own simply by getting the facts about flying and continuing to fly. It is more common, however, for the fear to escalate—even if you keep flying—if you do not engage in a rigorous self-help program or get help from a therapist.

The fear may also spread to other areas of your life. This is more likely to occur if your fear damages your self-esteem; that is, you begin to believe that you are a weak and worthless person because you cannot fly or fly with comfort. Whatever the mechanism, I have met dozens of people who started with a single fear, such as aviophobia or claustrophobia, and developed one or more other fears before they decided "enough is enough." I hope you will make this same decision now.

Summary

Factors related to the development of the fear of flying vary for each individual. Heredity, childhood environments, and faulty information play key roles in the development of phobias. Heredity and childhood environments are also implicated in the development of panic attacks, as are other factors, such as substance dependency and stressful lifestyles. It is not essential that you understand the causes of your fear to conquer it. It is essential that you replace your faulty information system with valid information and that you master the techniques that will be presented in the remainder of this book if you are to recover from your fear.

3

The Physiology of Fear

When you have a fearful response to a dangerous situation, your brain sends a signal to your hypothalamus gland to mobilize your body for action. The hypothalamus gland regulates your autonomic nervous system and controls such bodily functions as your heart and breathing. The result is that your body becomes mobilized for action to cope with the danger.

Let me illustrate what happens with a personal example. Recently, I was walking in the woods near my home when I had a very close encounter with a poisonous copperhead snake. My immediate response was to jump away from the snake to avoid the danger I perceived. The time between seeing the snake and reacting to it could be measured in tenths or hundredths of a second. While my response probably did not save my life, because copperhead bites are rarely fatal, it did save me a great deal of pain. You have probably had similar responses to danger, perhaps as you were driving on the freeway and the car or truck beside you suddenly swerved into your lane. Your response: get out of harm's way. That response may have saved your life, and this same response has saved countless millions of lives over the history of humankind.

This response to danger is called the fight-or-flight response. It is a normal and necessary part of human existence and has allowed us to continue to thrive as a species. All animals have it. However, the fight-or-flight response occurs in relation to perceived danger, whether the danger is real or imagined. When danger is real, the fight-or-flight response is useful. When the response is an exaggeration of danger—a phobic response—it must be controlled. The first step in controlling your physiological response to your exaggeration of the dangers posed by air travel is to understand what happens to your body. The primary purpose of this chapter is to further this understanding. You may wish to begin this journey of understanding by thinking about your last encounter with airplanes. My guess is that your response to planes was not much different from my response to the snake.

Before I discuss your automatic physical response to fearful thoughts, I want to address the idea of the controllability of these responses. Our heart beats and we breathe without conscious effort—that is, we do not have to remind our heart to beat and our breathing mechanism to work so we will have enough air. The physical response to fear also occurs automatically. The question that is often asked is, "If all of this occurs automatically, how can I influence my body?" You can influence these automatic responses by putting your conscious mind in "override" mode. In order to do this, you must learn how these responses occur and then use strategies that mental health professionals have used for decades to help people control their bodies. Let's begin by increasing your understanding of what happens to your body.

The Relationship Between Thoughts and Physical Responses

The beginning point of the fight-or-flight reaction is your thought. This idea is hard for some people to accept because of the short time between the perception that danger is at hand and the response to it. It may be useful to recall that scary thoughts about flying occur automatically, and any thoughts about flying will evoke them to some degree. For example, some fearful flyers have won their company's sales contest only to learn that their reward was an all expenses paid trip to Hawaii. The thought of flying to Hawaii brings on the fight-or-flight reaction even though they want to visit Hawaii.

What if you received a call telling you that you won first prize in a contest you entered, and the prize is airfare and hotel accommodations for a one-week stay in New York or San Francisco? That would probably result in immediate dread and a physical response. Imagine that you are driving by that airport on your way to work or a shopping mall and you look out your window and see a plane take off. What would your reaction be? Can you begin to feel your body respond to the danger? Have you ever agreed to take a friend to the airport and, as you approach the airport, begin to remember your last flying experience and start to get sweaty palms?

Thoughts about flying bring a physiological response that we know as the fight-or-flight reaction. It is brought on in the same way by thoughts about closed spaces if you are claustrophobic and by images of high spaces if you are acrophobic. When you change your thoughts about the things that scare you, this troublesome response will no longer occur.

The Physical Response to Fearful Thoughts: Before the Flight

Some people start having scary thoughts days, weeks, and even months prior to the actual flight. These thoughts produce anticipatory anxiety, and an entire chapter (Chapter 7) is devoted to this issue. Unless you learn to control your anticipatory anxiety, it is likely that you will stop flying. In a sense, because the flight is some time in the future, anticipatory anxiety can be characterized as the fear of fear. If the flight is several days away, there is obviously nothing that can harm you, but you worry about the "certain" danger associated with flying in the future.

When the fight is several days or weeks ahead, the thoughts about flying are often intermittent and involve momentary shortness of breath, memory loss, cold hands and feet, and muscle tension. If the anticipatory anxiety is intense, by which I mean that you have more or less continuous thoughts about flying, the physical symptoms can be severe. Migraine or tension headaches, lower back pain, diarrhea, and sleeplessness can occur. Other reactions to these thoughts include irritability, mental lapses such as forgetfulness, and bad dreams. In severe cases of anticipatory anxiety, people are totally miserable and are unable to sleep or even perform their jobs. In less severe cases of anticipatory anxiety, people are uncomfortable for short periods of time.

Bad Dreams

All fearful flyers who suffer from anticipatory anxiety have some physical reactions to their scary thought. Not all fearful fliers have dreams as a result of their anticipatory anxiety. However, when bad dreams (or nightmares) are a part of the response to anticipatory anxiety, some people interpret them as omens that something horrible is about to happen to them if they fly.

There are many theories about the meaning of dreams. My theory, which many mental health professionals share, is that when a problem exists, the brain continues to work on solving the problem as you sleep. Moreover, the responses you generate while you sleep do not differ greatly from those that surface when you are awake. The one difference between the waking responses and the sleeping responses is that the sleeping responses may be symbolic. Some fearful flyers do dream about airplane crashes. However, it seems more common for them to dream about disastrous outcomes involving dying, being maimed, the death of loved ones (which I believe represents the symbolic loss of their lives), and being chased by some awesome monster or beast (which I believe represents the airplane or death).

I will say it here and elsewhere in the book: one sure sign that you are recovering is that you no longer dream about disasters. In the meantime, do not interpret your bad dreams as omens that disaster is near. They are a natural, albeit uncomfortable, reaction to the fear.

Physical Responses to Flying: An In-Depth Look

Let's take an in-depth look at what happens to your body when you have an intense, fearful thought. As you know, this thought activates your body to respond to danger—flying. The moment the thought occurs, epinephrine, a hormone that mobilizes the entire body, is pumped into the bloodstream and several physiological events occur simultaneously. I'll describe these changes as they occur in the different parts of your body.

Cardiovascular Changes

Blood vessels constrict, blood pressure goes up, and your heartbeat increases dramatically, often going from a resting rate of 72 beats per minute to over 140 beats per minute. Also, the flow from your hands, feet, and brain to your central body cavity, and the composition of the blood changes because blood sugar increases. Blood sugar is pumped into the blood to fuel the physical reaction to the danger. The combined reactions of the cardiovascular system produce a symptom that actually increases the fear for many flyers. Because their hearts are beating so rapidly and seem to be out of control, many people fear they will have a heart attack.

A less pronounced result of the changes in the cardiovascular system is sweaty palms. The fact that palms start to sweat is paradoxical because the hands and feet actually get colder during the fight-or-flight reaction. Because the capillaries function differently in the mobilized state caused by a high level of epinephrine in the system, the palms do sweat, sometimes profusely.

Finally, some fearful flyers who suffer from a condition called *mitrovalve prolapse (MVP)* may find that it is worsened by the intense fight-or-flight response. Mitrovalve prolapse is a heart condition that is actually harmless. It is a problem that occurs mostly in women and is a mechanical abnormality that causes irregular heartbeat and heart palpitations. Irregular heartbeat and palpitations can, and often do, accelerate when people are experiencing stress. If you suffer from MVP and have not consulted your physician, please do so as soon as possible. A consultation will assure you that, even though you experience palpitations when you are flying, they are probably not dangerous.

Respiratory System

Your breathing also changes quite dramatically when you have intense fearful thoughts. Because your body requires more oxygen to fight or flee from the perceived danger, your breathing rate increases from its normal rate (six to fifteen breaths per minute) to twenty, thirty, or more breaths per minute. Not only does the rate change, but the way that you breathe changes. When you are relaxed, you breathe diaphragmatically; that is, the large muscles located under your rib cage (the diaphragm) operates your respiratory system to fill your lungs almost completely from the bottom up. When you are afraid, you breathe thoracically. The breathing action occurs in the upper part of your chest, which has the effect of quickly enriching your blood with oxygen and discarding (exhaling) carbon dioxide.

You can become aware of how you are breathing by placing your hand on your stomach just below your rib cage and breathe normally. If you are breathing diaphragmatically, your hand will rise when you inhale and fall when you exhale. Why? As your lungs fill during the inhale in the normal breathing process, they expand. As they expand they apply pressure to your stomach, which moves outward to make room for the enlarged lungs. The opposite reaction happens as you exhale, or let the air out of your lungs. Pay attention to your own breathing process for a few moments to familiarize yourself with how it feels. This knowledge is an essential first step toward taking control of the process.

What happens to your hands when you breathe thoracically? If you place one hand on your stomach, the other hand on your upper chest, and tense your abdominal muscles (those just over your stomach), you will get a sense of what happens when you breathe thoracically. Once you tense your stomach muscles, almost all movement will cease in the lower part of your chest, and the hand placed on the upper chest will begin to move. Also, you will probably note that your breathing rate increases if you continue to tense your abdominal muscles.

The result of the change in breathing that occurs when you breathe thoracically is not only that the blood becomes oxygen enriched, it also becomes carbon dioxide deficient, particularly when there is no physical activity to burn up the extra oxygen.

The Brain

Because of the fear, the presence of epinephrine, and the fact that some of the blood that is normally found in the cranial cavity surrounding the brain has been pumped into the part of the body that house the vital organs such as the heart, the brain functions quite differently. The brain actually shifts from the *cerebrum*—the center of the conscious thought—to what can best be termed the survival mode, and operates from a primitive part called the *brain stem*. Fearful flyers often report that before and during flights they cannot "think." This is actually a fairly accurate representation of what occurs. When you are intensely afraid, you are almost completely cut off from accessing information stored in the cerebrum, even if it was recently stored there. Many fearful flyers cannot remember what clothes they packed for the trip, are unable to find their car keys when they are ready to go to the airport, and are totally unable to perform even the most basic cognitive tasks such as preparing for a business meeting.

Finally, because of the shortage of carbon dioxide that results from the change in breathing, certain portions of the brain produce dizziness. If this shortage of carbon dioxide is severe and prolonged, you will pass out. This is the body's way of taking over the breathing process and restoring the oxygen-carbon dioxide balance. Remember that if you get dizzy and pass out, you are experiencing a shortage of carbon dioxide, not a deficit of oxygen, as most people believe. This shortage of carbon dioxide also produces one of the scariest symptoms associated with the fear of flying—a choking sensation that seems very much like you are suffocating. This is particularly disconcerting for people who suffer from claustrophobia because they expect to experience a lack of air in closed spaces. In the chapter that follows you will learn how to recognize this response and cope with it.

Muscles

Muscles tense in response to the perceived fear. If the fear is short in duration, the tension will dissipate quite quickly. However, if you have anticipatory anxiety and then take a long plane trip, muscle tension can produce a great deal of discomfort and even severe pain. The *temporo-mandibular joint (TMJ)*, which is located at the point where the lower jaw is fastened to the skull, the *trapezius muscles,* which are located on top of the shoulders, the muscles in the lower back, and the muscles in the calves and legs seem most problematic in this regard. One of the most common sights in our seminars for fearful flyers was participants rubbing their backs and the tops of their shoulders by noon on the first day. If you find yourself massaging your shoulders, suffering from lower back pain, or tapping your foot, the muscle tension has reached the point where you need to take charge of it.

Muscle tension produces some symptoms other than tension and pain. One of these is uncontrollable shaking, particularly of the legs. Some fearful flyers are so embarrassed about their legs shaking that they carry jackets to place over their legs so others will not notice the shaking. Another symptom, which results from a combination of factors includes muscle tension, is that the legs seem so weak they will not provide the needed support. Some fearful flyers will not get out of their seats because they are afraid that they will collapse in the aisle. This will not happen!

Finally, as muscle tension builds, some fearful flyers become so distraught that they fear they will attack a flight attendant or literally throw open the emergency exits while the plane is in flight. So far as I know, a fearful flyer has never attacked a flight attendant, or anyone else on an airplane. And don't worry about opening the emergency exits while you are in flight. It is impossible for you to open the plug-type doors and windows that make up the safety exits. As the plane is pressurized, the pressure of those exits increases to the point that an entire professional football team pulling simultaneously with all their strength would be unable to open them. It was the case at one time that some planes were equipped with rear exits that could be opened in flight. After a bank robber forced a flight attendant to open one of these exits in flight and parachuted from the plane, these exits were equipped with external locks that close automatically once the plane is airborne.

Vision

A few fearful flyers experience blurred vision, primarily because the presence of too much oxygen in the bloodstream causes the pupils of the eyes to dilate. One person reported that this persisted after the flight, probably because she had "flashbacks," which created intense physical reactions. Paradoxically, at the onset of the fight-or-flight reaction, you can see somewhat better because of your heightened physical state.

Hearing

One of the reactions to your fear is that your hearing improves. A result of this, and your heightened physical and psychological states, is that you can hear the mechanical sounds of the aircraft much better than people who are not afraid. Many fearful flyers report asking the person sitting next to them if they heard a sound that they were certain was an engine exploding, only to learn that the person heard nothing.

Gastrointestinal Reactions

Your stomach may become upset because, as a reaction to your fear, the lining secretes more acid. In addition, when you breathe rapidly and shallowly, you can draw more air into your stomach—a condition not unlike what occurs when babies cry. When these two conditions occur together or separately, they can upset your stomach. Lower gastrointestinal distress can also occur in the form of diarrhea.

Medication, Alcohol, and the Reaction to Fear

Many people came to our seminars grasping a variety of medications, including Valium, Xanax, Klonipin, and Ativan, all of which are anti-anxiety medications. One person came "equipped" with ten small bottles of vodka. Some of the people who brought medication had not taken it before. In preparing for the seminar, they visited their physicians, who in turn prescribed medication. Others had taken medication before, but found that it did not produce the results they desired. Many enrollees had used (and abused) alcohol to help them fly, including some who were nondrinkers except when they flew. In a few instances, the abuse of alcohol had been so great people had become alcoholics. When these people came to terms with their drinking, they no longer had the crutch that allowed them to fly.

I am not against using anti-anxiety medication as one tool to help you overcome your fear of flying (with one exception, which I will discuss in the next paragraph). I am against the use of medication and alcohol as the sole tool in your effort to deal with your fear. Why? First, neither alcohol nor anti-anxiety medication are curative, which means you will have to rely on them for the rest of your life if they are your only weapon against fear. Second, if you are intensely afraid, medication and alcohol will be of no use to you unless you are prepared to take them in large doses and actually knock yourself out. Third, the medications listed at the beginning of the section and alcohol are addictive. An addiction to some of the medications, such as Xanax, can develop in as little as a week of continuous use. Moreover, once you become addicted to Xanax and some of the other drugs, it takes at least thirty days for withdrawal to occur as you gradually wean yourself from them. Many physicians fail to tell their patients about the addictiveness of these medications.

There is one exception to my endorsement of the use of anti-anxiety drugs to overcome the fear of flying: if you have ever been addicted to drugs or alcohol, my best advice is to avoid the use of drugs as a part of your treatment. Drugs may make the process a bit easier, but you run the risk of trading one problem (the fear of flying) for another (an addiction to drugs).

How does the body react to drugs and alcohol when you are afraid? Recall that all of the physical reactions to the fear begin with the perception that you are in danger. These thoughts produce the physical responses already described—responses that have developed over the course of our evolution to allow us to cope with danger. What happens when you take an anti-anxiety medication or drink an alcoholic drink when you are afraid? The immediate response is relaxation, because alcohol and anti-anxiety medications depress heart rate and slow breathing. The brain, recognizing that your body is no longer ready to deal with the danger, pumps more epinephrine into your bloodstream, which in turn stimulates the heart, tenses the muscles, and alters your breathing. If you take another pill or absorb another drink, the brain increases the level of epinephrine in your bloodstream again. And so it goes, until the alcohol or medication level in your bloodstream is so overpowering that you pass out or are numb.

You must be the judge of whether drugs are a solution to your fear. I have heard reports of people with mild, sporadic fear who were much more comfortable after one drink or a quarter-milligram xanex pill. However, these reports seem to be the exceptions. Other fearful flyers report drinking as many as a dozen cocktails in two hours with no lessening of fear. Another flyer took six quarter-milligram xanex pills and drank seven cocktails in three hours and experienced no reduction in his physical or cognitive response. In my view the twin risks of addiction and failure are too great to allow either "self-medication" via alcohol or physician-pre-scribed medication to serve as your primary defense against the fear of flying.

Identifying Your Symptoms

Chapter 4 will give you strategies to control all of your thoughts as well as your physical reactions to your fear. Later, in Chapter 7, after you have developed a valid information base about flying, you will be give tech-niques for dealing with anticipatory anxiety. However, in order to take advantage of the material in these chapters, you must identify your physi-cal reactions to fear. The table that follows is a checklist of symptoms experienced by fearful flyers. Please go through this list carefully and identify the symptoms you experience as a result of your fear. As you go through the checklist of symptoms, mark all of your reactions to your fear.

Symptoms Produced by the Fear of Flying

Brain Functioning

_____   racing, irrational thoughts (1,8)

_____   forgetfulness—short-term memory loss (1)

_____   dizziness (2)

_____   out of body experience; observing one's self (2)

_____   passing out (2)

_____   concentration is impossible (1,2)

_____   cannot speak coherently (1,2)

Cardiovascular System

_____   racing heart (2,3)

_____   palpitations/irregular heartbeat (MVP) (5,6)

Respiratory Symptoms

_____   tightness in throat and chest (2)

_____ rapid breathing/panting (2)

_____ can't get a full breath (2)

Vision

_____ blurred vision (2)

Hearing

_____ fear heightened by mechanical sounds (2)

Muscles

_____ discomfort in the TMJ, trapezius, or other muscles (4)

_____ legs shaking uncontrollably (4)

_____ feeling uncoordinated (4)

_____ urge to hit someone or "tear open" the exits (1,2,4)

_____ bite nails, tap foot, or other nervous habit (2,4)

Stomach/Intestines

_____ butterflies, queasiness (2)

_____ vomiting (1,2,7)

_____ diarrhea (1,2,7)

_____ eat all the time or not at all (2,4,7)

Other Symptoms

_____ hands and feet get cold (2)

_____ face flushes (2)

_____ palms perspiring (2)

_____ tingling or numbing in hands, lips, or other parts (2)

The numbers in the checklist represent strategies for controlling the symptoms listed:

   1 = Thought stopping

2 = Breathing techniques

3 = Valsalva maneuver

4 = Muscle relaxation techniques

5 = See a doctor

6 = Take medication

7 = Techniques for anticipatory anxiety (see Chapter 7)

8 = Valid information base

For example, racing irrational thoughts can be controlled by a combination of thought stopping (1) and a valid information base (8) about flying. You must understand why planes are able to fly, that the air traffic control system is safe, and that generally you are much more likely to die in your automobile or a taxi as you drive across town. A (2) next to a symptom, such as feet and hand getting cold, indicates that it can be controlled by breathing techniques designed to return your breathing to normal. A racing heart can be slowed either by controlling your breathing (2) or the Valsalva maneuver (3). Actually, there are several strategies that can be employed to slow a racing heart, and you will need to learn one of these if you are concerned about this problem.

Some symptoms can be controlled by the use of deep muscle relaxation strategies. These have a (4) beside them. If you have mitrovalve prolapse, you should see a physician (5) and you may require medication (6). Because some problems develop as a result of anticipatory anxiety, they can only be dealt with by eliminating or reducing this part of your problem (7).

All of the strategies mentioned here will be described in detail in subsequent chapters. The important point for you at this time is that all of your symptoms can be controlled. It is up to you to learn how to control them.

Back to Thoughts

The symptoms listed in the table are caused by catastrophic thoughts about flying. Unfortunately, the symptoms also give rise to other scary thoughts that heighten the fear. I have already noted that a rapid heartbeat causes some fearful flyers to think they will have a heart attack. Tightness in the throat and chest can cue thoughts about suffocation, just as mechanical sounds can initiate thoughts of falling and crashes. The physical symptoms resulting from fear are bad enough to endure in and of themselves, but sometimes the thoughts they spawn are unbearable.

However, there is some good new in all of this: there are several points at which you may stop or reduce your fear of flying. One of these is by stopping the catastrophic thoughts. Eliminating or controlling the physical symptoms produced by those scary thoughts is another point at which you can gain control of your fear. Physical symptoms such as a racing heart increase the feeling of being out of control, a feeling that is unacceptable for many people who are afraid to fly. The ability to slow your heart rate, control your breathing, and reduce your muscle tension will restore your belief that you are in control of your body, which can be tremendously empowering. It is also important for you to know that you can control the physical symptoms even if your mind races. I have seen people do it.

Your goal should be to replace the catastrophic thoughts with rational beliefs about flying and to control any physical symptoms that arise. To rid yourself of this fear, you must learn to control both your thoughts and your physical responses, but learning to do one is not necessarily linked to the other. This is very important for you to know if you are a fearful flyer who hates the physical symptoms you experience when you fly.

Summary

Scary, catastrophic thoughts bring on the fight-or-flight reaction. The heart races, breathing becomes rapid and shallow, and muscles tense to prepare you to deal with your own monster, an airplane. The symptoms that the fear produces give rise to other even scarier thoughts in many instances. Fortunately, the thoughts and physical symptoms can be controlled by rather simple techniques. These strategies and their application to the fear of flying will be described in subsequent chapters.

4

Techniques for Coping
with the Fear

What is curative? How can you rid yourself of this despicable problem that interferes with your life? By eliminating your anticipatory anxiety (Chapter 7), by compiling an accurate database about flying to replace your current beliefs (Chapters 5 and 6), and by coping with your fear on the plane. Once you learn that you can control your thoughts, your muscle tension, your heart rate, and your breathing, planes will be less frightening. If you can recall the information presented in Chapters 5 and 6 while cruising at 35,000 feet or when the plane is in turbulence, your fear will either be gone or minimized to the point that you will have only one thought, "I can fly."

In order to reach the point of being able to control your thoughts, you must learn the techniques discussed in this chapter. In addition, you must learn to "measure" your fear so you know whether you are making any progress. The first section in this chapter teaches you how to measure your fear.

Measuring Your Fear

You can measure your fear using what Joseph Wolpe calls a SUDS (Subjective Units of Disturbance Scale) in his book *The Practice of Behavior*

Therapy (4th ed. New York: Pergammon, 1990). This scale is *subjective* because it is your measure of your fear, and no one else's. It would be a *normative* scale if it compared your fear response with the responses to other people. To begin, I want you to think about a time when you are perfectly relaxed. For some people this is the time just before dropping off to sleep. For others it is lying on the beach listening to the sound of the surf and sea birds. That is a 1 on your subjective scale. Now think about a time when you are most scared, when you are at the maximum level of your tolerance for fear. This represents 100 on your SUDS scale and means that you are intensely afraid, as scared as you can get. Your SUDS score may never have been to 100 on an airplane, but if you have the active imagination of most fearful flyers, you can imagine yourself at this point. A 50 on your SUDS scale is the halfway point between being perfectly relaxed and totally frightened.

Begin now to learn to measure your fear by thinking about your last flight. On a scale of 1 to 100, how frightened were you at each step in the flight? What was your SUDS score when you were going to the airport? During takeoff? While cruising? During landing? Fill in your score for each of these on the table shown below.

As you work on conquering your fear, continue to use your SUDS score to measure the intensity. You will also be using your SUDS score as a partial basis for establishing goals for your graduation flight. This process is described in Chapter 9. Finally, and most importantly, you will be using your SUDS score to determine whether the techniques described in

Using Your SUDS Scale to Measure Fear

		Going to Airport	Takeoff	Cruise	Descent/ Landing
Totally frightened	100				
Moderately frightened	50				
Totally relaxed	1				

the subsequent sections of this chapter actually work. If they do, and I know that they work, you can lower your SUDS score while you are actually flying. When that occurs, you will begin to get a sense that you can control your response to your fear.

Stopping Racing Thoughts

You now know that once the fear develops, the catastrophic thoughts about flying are automatic. In fact, they seem to be premonitions about your flight. They are not. Almost everyone who took the fear of flying seminars had premonitions about headlines in the local newspapers reading, "Fearful Flyer Class Dies in Fiery Crash!" Others had thoughts about having panic attacks, embarrassing themselves in the plane, and suffocating in that "tiny tube" (the fuselage of the airplane).

Perhaps the worst thoughts are those that begin when the door is about to be closed, such as, I'll be trapped with no place to go for the next two hours, I'll die and never see my children again, or we'll hit turbulence, and the plane will spiral out of control, and we'll all die! All of these thoughts must be stopped, but how?

Before I answer this question, please remember that the thoughts are automatic and ignoring them will do little good. You must take direct, assertive action to deal with the fearful thoughts that come to you. *Thought stopping* is a simple but effective technique that involves five steps:

1. Identify the scary thought and decide that you do not want it anymore.

2. Snap yourself in the palm of your hand with a sturdy rubber band. This will hurt!

3. Tell yourself to stop thinking those thoughts, using your native language.

4. Remind yourself, "I can handle my fear."

5. Repeat steps 1 through 4 as often as necessary.

Step One: Identify Irrational Thoughts

The thoughts that come to you about flying are for the most part irrational. They are exaggerations of the things that are likely to occur on airplanes. The reason that they scare you is because you believe the false message:

FEAR = False Evidence Appearing to be Real

You need to reframe this as:

FEAR = Forget Everything And Recover.

To do this you must recognize the irrational thought and actively decide that you want to dismiss it. In effect you are saying, "I choose to dismiss you."

Step Two: Interrupt Irrational Thoughts

On the day of the flight, place a rubber band around your hand so that it is positioned just over the palm. Choose a thick rubber band that fits snugly over your hand but does not cut off the circulation. A thick rubber band is sturdier and thus will not break with repeated use. (Yes, you may have to use it several times.) Thick rubber bands are preferred to thin ones for another reason. Believe it or not, the thicker rubber bands do not sting as much as the thin ones. I tested this "theory" one day in a large office supply store. I proceeded to snap the palms of my hands with various types of rubber bands while several people looked at me as though I had gone over the edge.

What happens when you snap yourself with a rubber band? It hurts! It stings! More importantly, it interrupts the racing thoughts that drive you off the plane or that make you uncomfortable on the plane.

Step Three: Counterattack Irrational Thoughts

The next step in thought stopping is to issue an injunction to yourself to stop thinking those irrational thoughts. This order to yourself should be sharp and decisive, and if you can muster it, accompanied by anger directed at your fear, never at yourself. This order to stop should come from your own self-talk, and for most people, should be in their first language. So in Spanish you would say, "Para!" The one exception that I have encountered to using your native language as the basis for injunctions is French. It simply takes too long to say stop in French according to French-speaking people who have used this technique. If your first language is French, you may not find this to be the case.

Think for a moment how you talk to yourself. Are there single words or brief phrases that you use to stop thought patterns in your day-to-day life? These might be effective in stopping your irrational thoughts about flying. Do you swear in your self-talk? Some people find it easier to conjure up anger at their fear if they swear at "it." Your injunction should be something brief and decisive that is not a personal putdown. Remember, you weaken your ability to cope with your fear when you engage in self-criticism.

If you cannot come up with an injunction of your own, try some of the following ones that have been used successfully by people like you:

- "Stop this s---."

- "Deborah! Stop!" (Substitute your name, using your mother's voice.)

- "In your face."

- "No more."

- "Enough already!"

- "Cut the crap."

- "Quit."

- "Damn you!" (Like phantom of the opera.)

Generating anger to accompany the injunction is difficult for many people. Some people cannot imagine themselves being aggressive with their fear because it seems so powerful. Also, some people never permit themselves to feel anger for any reason, and this can be a barrier to being angry with their fear. It may be useful for you to make another list of the costs associated with your fear, or review the list you made in Chapter 1, as a means of getting in touch with your anger. What has your fear cost you in terms of money? Lost jobs? Canceled flights? Lost opportunities to make money, such as taking a promotion? What has it cost you in terms of relationships? Missed family reunions, graduations, baptisms, bar mitzvahs? What has it cost you in terms of fun? Missed vacations? Being with friends and family? The costs associated with the fear of flying are often astronomical when put in terms of money, relationships, and fun. Finally, it is okay to feel anger, particularly if it is for a good cause. What better cause could there be than defeating your fear of flying?

Larry, a SWAT team member on a large metropolitan police force, had always called himself terrible names because he was afraid to fly. He had vivid memories of his panic attacks, which he was sure would reoccur if he flew. When he redirected his anger and started calling his fear names instead of himself, he turned the corner and began to fly. You can too!

Step Four: Use Positive Self-Talk

"I can" or power statements should follow the injunction to yourself to stop. When you tell yourself that you *can* do something, you are affirming that you have the techniques and personal strength necessary to do it. In the case of flying you are telling yourself that you can handle your fear and fly. Self-affirming positive statements, like injunctions, need to be brief and to the point.

In order to develop your positive self-statement, you may need to review your strengths. Identify any adversity that you have overcome and any triumphs in your personal or career world. Then develop a statement such as those developed by triumphant fearful flyers before you. One woman related that she had climbed to the top of a male-dominated organization over untold opposition. She said, "I know what they say about me behind my back: 'She's one tough bitch,' and they are right." That phrase, as distasteful as it might be to some, became a part of her master plan to overcome another obstacle: fear of flying. Some of the following positive self-statements may help you write your own:

- "I can handle this!"
- "I *can!!!*" (visualized)
- "I've done harder things."
- "I'm stronger than my fear."
- "My fear can't stop me."
- "I can defeat my fear."

A few people cannot imagine themselves being strong and thus cannot come up with statements affirming their personal power. If you are one of these people, replace the affirming self-statement with a motivational statement in your thought-stopping strategy. This motivational statement should reflect your reason for wanting to overcome your fear. One woman, who had never flown, wanted to join her husband in Paris to celebrate their thirtieth wedding anniversary. Her motivational statement was, "I'll see Paris when I conquer my fear." My favorite motivational statement comes from dozens of people who had conquered many fears, but were still hampered by their fear of flying. They often used, "When I fly, I'll be free!" By this they meant free of crippling fears.

Barriers to Using Thought Stopping

You must overcome three major barriers if you are to use thought stopping successfully. First, it is painful, and many people say, "I'm not into pain." Yes you are, if you tolerate your fear of flying. Think of all the psychological pain you endure because of your fear. You have certainly been scared, which is painful. You may have been humiliated when you got off a plane at the last moment. Is that not painful? What about the loneliness you have experienced because you missed a vacation, wedding, or family get-together? The momentary pain you will experience as a result of snapping yourself with a rubber band is nothing compared to what you have already endured.

The second barrier is the embarrassment that some people feel when they snap themselves. They are concerned that other people may notice and think that they are weird. These people are typically what I call the "cool fearful flyer." They give no external signs of being afraid, even when they are terrified. Recall that I stood in an office supply store and snapped myself with numerous rubber bands while more than one person gave me an "inquisitive" look. It was a bit embarrassing.

You must be able to do two things in order get over your embarrassment. The first of these is to give yourself permission to take some risks while you are recovering from your fear. Taking risks means doing some things that are out of the ordinary for you. The second thing that you must do is use your sense of humor. One fearful flyer, who was riding in first class, told a seatmate that the rubber band he was wearing was a Rolex accessory, a story made somewhat credible by the presence of a $20,000 Rolex on his left wrist. Another flyer related that her color-coordinated rubber band was a new European fashion accessory. Never mind that she bought it at the local quick-stop, and that if you turned it over it read, "Fly Crazy." If none of these techniques appeals to you, my best advice is, when you snap the rubber band and your seatmate looks at you inquisitively or judgmentally, lean over and whisper, "If I don't snap this thing once in a while, I throw up." I can personally guarantee that the person sitting next to you will be delighted to have you snap your rubber band. Don't be surprised if they try to help you snap it!

The third barrier to using thought stopping is the superstitious belief that thinking irrational thoughts keeps the plane in the air. This belief goes something like this: it is true that you have flown in the past and worried, and the plane arrived safely. You may even have "helped" it by listening to every sound, counting the screws on the wings to see if any were missing, watching the faces of the flight attendants for any sign of panic, looking out the window for other planes that might be on a collision course with your plane, and so forth.

Unfortunately, your hypervigilant behavior became linked to the safe arrival of the plane, and now giving up those thoughts scares you even more. I can only assure you that you had nothing to do with the plane arriving safely. I know that when you are not gripped by fear, you would agree that it is impossible for a relatively small person sitting inside the plane to hold up a modern jetliner that may weigh from 100,000 to 1,000,000 pounds. The air traffic control system and the onboard traffic and collision avoidance system keep the planes apart, not your watchful behavior. Decide now to give up these irrational thoughts.

Review of Thought Stopping

Thought stopping takes less than three seconds. You recognize your fear, decide that you do not want it, snap your rubber band, tell yourself to stop thinking these thoughts, and remind yourself that you can handle your fear and air travel (or use your motivational statement). How often you have to use thought stopping depends on many things, including how practiced you become in using the coping strategies discussed in this chapter. Thought stopping is one technique, but it must be used in conjunction with other strategies to be effective.

Controlling Your Breathing

As you learned in Chapter 3, when you have scary thoughts, your brain prepares your body to do battle by pumping epinephrine into your bloodstream. One of the immediate changes is that you breathe faster and shallower. This throws off carbon dioxide and pumps more oxygen into your bloodstream. The result is you may experience a choking sensation in your throat, light-headedness, and dizziness. This process is 100 percent controllable. In fact, you must control it in order to restore both your body's and brain's functioning to normal. You should begin to control your breathing the moment you recognize the scary thought, snap your rubber band, tell yourself to stop thinking those thoughts, and affirm that you can handle your fear.

The RED Technique

Of the many techniques that can be used to control breathing, I recommend one I call the RED technique. It gets its name from your control of the rate, exhale, and diaphragm. Your goal should be to breathe less than twenty times per minute, control the exhale so that you always exhale very slowly, and to fill your lungs from the bottom using the diaphragm, the large muscle just under your rib cage. But how do you do this?

The moment after you snap your rubber band, begin to inhale, forcing yourself to breathe from your diaphragm and thus fill your lungs from the bottom. To be sure you are breathing from the diaphragm, place your hand on your stomach just below the rib cage and push in when you inhale. Time your inhale by counting: one thousand one, one thousand two, one thousand three. At the count of one thousand three, stop breathing and hold your breath. As you hold your breath, count one thousand one, one thousand two, one thousand three. At this point purse your lips as though you are going to kiss your sister and begin to exhale through your lips, again counting one thousand one, one thousand two, one thousand three.

Now comes the hard part. After you have expelled the air from your lungs on the exhale, stop breathing, by which I mean rest, neither inhaling nor exhaling. As you do, count one thousand one, one thousand two, one thousand three. Once you reach one thousand three, you are ready to begin the process all over again. Here are the steps again:

1. Inhale and count one thousand one, one thousand two, one thousand three. (Push on your stomach just below the rib cage as a reminder to force the diaphragm to work.)

2. Hold your breath and count one thousand one, one thousand two, one thousand three.

3. Purse your lips and exhale. Count one thousand one, one thousand two, one thousand three.

4. Rest (this will be hard) and count one thousand one, one thousand two, one thousand three.

5. Repeat for five to seven minutes.

If the process of controlling your breathing sounds easy, it is, except for two parts. When you start the process, you will find that you want to inhale very quickly, because your brain is telling you that you are suffocating. It is lying to you, and you must teach it that you have a shortage of carbon dioxide and an *oversupply* of oxygen. That is why you get lightheaded and feel the choking sensation. The second difficult point will be when you are supposed to rest at the end of the first cycle. Because it takes a few minutes for the symptoms associated with hyperventilating to subside, your brain will tell you that you are still suffocating. Don't believe it!

It may help you combat the fear of suffocation if you remind yourself that the worst thing that can happen if you hyperventilate is that you will pass out. Then your body takes over, you breathe normally, and the oxygen-carbon dioxide balance is restored. You wake up, and though you may be a little embarrassed, you will be fine.

The RED technique slows your breathing to twelve to fifteen times a minute, forces you to control the exhale, and employs the diaphragm in the breathing process. In five to seven minutes, much of your body's functioning will be restored to normal, including your heart rate and the temperature of your hands. You will also find that you can get in touch with the rational part of your brain. If you have acquired the knowledge to offset your misinformation about flying, you can combat your scary thoughts using accurate information.

If Light-Headedness Does Not Go Away

I have seen hundreds of people use the RED technique to control their bodily response to fear while they were flying. A few of these people reported difficulty in totally eliminating the light-headed feeling. This is typically because the muscles involved in breathing have not become completely relaxed. There are three sets of muscles that can become so tense they interfere with normal breathing: the muscles in the chest, the diaphragm, and for some people, the throat muscles. If you are using the RED technique and you are still light-headed, relaxing these three sets of muscles will help.

Identify, Tense, Relax

In order to relax tense muscles, you locate the source of the tenseness (identify); increase the tension tense for five seconds (one thousand one, one thousand two, one thousand three, one thousand four, one thousand five); and release the tension in the muscle (relax). At the same time, you cue the relaxation process by mentally saying, "relax." If you can visualize the word *relax*, or use another visual cue such as a relaxing scene, it may increase your relaxation. Repeat this process three to five times on each muscle group.

For the muscle groups involved in breathing, the following "coach class" exercises are recommended. Why coach class? Because you will be doing them on an airplane, and most of us sit in coach class. To practice at home, use a dining room chair and imagine that people are sitting on either side.

First, concentrate on the muscles in the chest.

1. Square your shoulders and lift your hands into a fighting position. Do not clench your fists!

2. Now, try to touch your elbows behind your back. When you have forced your elbows as far toward each other as you can, hold the tension that develops in the chest muscles and count one thousand one, one thousand two, one thousand three.

3. Tell yourself, "relax," and release the tension by moving your hands toward each other. Let the tension flow from your chest as you relax.

4. Repeat three to five times or until the muscles in the chest area are relaxed.

Next relax the diaphragm. This will be difficult and will cause some discomfort.

1. Imagine that you are about to pull the skin on your stomach up under your rib cage (which is the part of your body that is just above your stomach. It contains your lungs).

2. Now begin to suck your stomach *in* and *up* under your ribs. When you have pulled as much of your skin in and up as possible, hold the tension and count one thousand one, one thousand two, one thousand three, one thousand four, one thousand five.

3. Release the tension and tell yourself, "relax," and let the tension flow from the stomach.

4. Repeat until light-headedness dissipates.

If your throat muscles constrict when you become frightened, use the following exercise to relax.

1. Point your chin toward the ceiling, stretching the throat muscles as much as you can in this manner.

2. Place your tongue in the roof of your mouth and push with your tongue as hard as you can. Count one thousand one, one thousand two, one thousand three, one thousand four, one thousand five.

3. Release the pressure being applied by your tongue and lower your chin, telling yourself to relax as you do.

4. Repeat three to five times, or until the tension in your throat muscles has dissipated.

For most people, using the RED technique will eliminate the light-headedness that results from the body's reaction to fearful thoughts. If it does not totally eliminate it, be prepared to use these coach class relaxation exercises to increase your comfort.

Plan B

I recommend the RED technique for controlling your breathing, but there is one more breathing strategy you can use with ease. In the seatback pocket in front of your seat on the airplane, there will be a small white bag that is placed there in case people get airsick. If your lightheadedness continues, just place that bag over your nose and mouth, hold it tightly so no air comes in from the outside, and breathe normally. This will restore the oxygen-carbon dioxide balance in a matter of minutes. Why? After you breathe into the bag for a few minutes you are breathing almost pure carbon dioxide.

The bag works, but most people are too embarrassed to use it. However, one desperate flier put it this way, "If that's all I have to do to get rid of those dizzy feelings, I don't give a damn what the other people on the plane think." Most fearful fliers will not allow themselves the luxury of not caring what others think.

Review of Controlling Your Breathing

You should begin to control your breathing the moment you finish with thought stopping. When you control your breathing, it signals the rest of the body that everything is okay, and the body responds. You control your breathing by taking over the automatic response generated by the brain and placing your breathing on manual override using the RED technique. Employing the RED technique is as simple as counting one thousand one, one thousand two, one thousand three four times. During this process you must ignore the false information that comes from your brain that you are suffocating. It's a lie!

Finally, if you do not become comfortable after five to seven minutes, relax the muscles involved in the breathing process to increase your comfort.

Slowing a Racing Heart

Whenever you have those automatic, scary thoughts about what is going to happen to you as you fly, one physical reaction is a racing heart, which means that your heart rate may increase by two or three times its normal rate. The good news is that, if you have good cardiovascular health, it could beat at this rate for days without injury to your heart. And there is more good news: the RED technique will slow a racing heart. However, all this good news may not be sufficient if you are one of the people who first gets frightened by air travel, only to have that fear heightened by the fear that your heart is literally going to burst because it is pounding so hard. Many people have described the way they feel as, "It seemed that my heart was going to come out of my chest."

The Valsalva Maneuver

You can immediately slow your racing heart by using a technique called the Valsalva maneuver, after the physiologist who discovered it. Actually, Valsalva discovered a whole family of techniques to slow the racing heart, but only one of them is described here because it can be used easily and unobtrusively on an airplane.

Cautions

Two cautions are in order. First, this technique is only for people who have healthy cardiovascular systems. Why? Because the Valsalva maneuver can stop your heart altogether if you have a diseased cardiovascular system. It works by stimulating the *vegus nerve*, which regulates heart rate and runs the length of the body. If your cardiovascular system is diseased, the maneuver may stop the heart.

If you have any doubts about your health in this area, consult your physician. He or she may be able to recommend a similar technique that will work for you. Although mitrovalve prolapse does not constitute a cardiovascular problem, I still recommend that you talk to your physician prior to using the Valsalva maneuver or any strategy that influences your cardiovascular system simply because it will increase your confidence that what you are doing will not injure you.

Second, I caution you that while the Valsalva maneuver will lower your heart rate, it must be used with the RED breathing technique if you are going to maintain the gains you get from using it. The epinephrine that causes the heart rate to increase is still in your system, and controlling your breathing will allow your body to eliminate it from your system.

How It Works

Everything begins with frightening thoughts, which set the physical symptoms in motion. When the thoughts come, your heart rate will increase instantaneously to 120 or 150 beats per minute. You decide that you want to lower your heart rate. To do this:

1. Sit erect in your coach class seat.

2. Force yourself to fill your lungs to capacity just as you did in the first step of the RED technique.

3. As you are filling your lungs, tuck in your tummy—that is, flatten it by pulling it in and up. Do not go as far as you did when you relaxed your diaphragm.

4. When your lungs are totally filled, hold your breath. Using your stomach muscles, push down on your lower stomach (intestines) for five seconds much as you would if you were constipated. As you are pushing, count one thousand one, one thousand two, one thousand three, one thousand four, one thousand five.

5. Release the tension and exhale. Your heart rate will immediately come down about twenty beats per minute.

6. Repeat the process. You will need to repeat it three to four times. Once you are comfortable with your heart rate, immediately use the RED technique to control your breathing. If you do not, your heart rate will accelerate again.

Relaxing Tense Muscles

The process of relaxing tense muscles in your chest, diaphragm, and throat was described in "Controlling Your Breathing" and will not be repeated here. However, other muscle groups may become so tense that you need to apply the identify, tense, relax process. These muscle groups are the shoulder muscles and those at the base of the head and neck, which can be relaxed using the Turtle; the temporomandibular joint (TMJ), that links your lower jaw to the upper jaw, which can be relaxed using the Piranha; and the upper legs and calves, which can be relaxed using the Ballerina.

The Turtle

The trapezius muscles are the large muscles on the shoulders that support the neck. They, along with the muscles at the base of the skull, are "stress susceptible," as are the other muscle groups discussed in this section. Fortunately, it is fairly easy to relax the shoulder muscles using the following exercise, which I call the Turtle.

1. Sit erect in your coach class seat.

2. Simultaneously shrug your shoulders and pull in your neck like a turtle would do if he were pulling his heads into his shell. Try as hard as you can to pull your head in and touch your ears with the tops of your shoulders. Make your neck disappear.

3. Hold the tension and as you count, one thousand one, one thousand two, one thousand three, one thousand four, one thousand five, rotate your head back and around to massage the muscles in your shoulders.

4. Release the tension at the count of five and tell yourself to relax. Just let your shoulder muscles fall back into a normal position and feel the muscle tension drain away.

5. Repeat three to five times or until the neck and shoulder muscles are soft and relaxed.

The Piranha

The Turtle is also a good exercise to use if you get tense while driving. So is the Piranha. The TMJ can get so tense that it requires medication to relax in some instances. However, you can relax it by pretending you are a fish with an overbite, the Piranha.

1. Start by extending your lower jaw as far as you can forward, trying to extend it beyond the teeth in the upper jaw.

2. When you have extended it as far as you can, count one thousand one, one thousand two, one thousand three, one thousand four, one thousand five.

3. Release the tension, tell yourself to relax, and let the jaw return to its normal position.

4. Repeat three to five times.

The Ballerina

The muscles in the upper and lower legs frequently become very tense before and during a flight. I have seen the tension result in uncontrollable shaking of the legs. Even in this condition, your legs will support you if you need to walk around. However, you can take control of the tension by doing another coach class exercise, the Ballerina. If you have ever watched a dancer, particularly a ballet dancer, warm up, you know they go through extensive stretching exercises to prepare their bodies for the rigors of dancing. In one of these exercises they point the toe away from themselves and then rotate the foot to point it toward themselves. This is exactly what you do in the Ballerina.

1. Slide your feet under the seat in front of you. There is not much room so the feet will have to stay near the floor. Remember, this is a coach class exercise.

2. Now, lift one foot just off the floor, arch your foot and point it away from you toward the front of the airplane (this will tense the large muscles on the top of the leg). Count, one thousand one thousand two, one thousand three, one thousand four, one thousand five.

3. Now rotate your foot so that your toe is pointing toward you (this will stretch the muscles along the back of the leg all the way to the buttocks). Try to point your foot at your chin and, as you do, count one thousand one, one thousand two, one thousand three, one thousand four, one thousand five.

4. Now tell yourself to relax. Allow your foot to drop to the floor of the plane and repeat with the other leg.

5. Repeat three to five times with each leg.

The Ballerina will allow you to relax the tension in your legs to some degree. However, if this tension gets painful and this technique is not working, go to the rear of the plane in the lavatory area and do some regular stretching exercises. The walk will be good for you because it will give you a sense of mastery over your environment. The exercises will help you relieve the tension, and this too will increase your feeling of being in control.

Which Techniques Will You Use?

I have described a technique to stop your racing thoughts; one that can be used to control your breathing (actually two if you count the paper bag); a strategy that, when used with the RED technique, can be used to slow a racing heart; and the identify, tense, relax technique that can be used to alleviate muscle tension. Which ones will you use? It depends entirely upon your symptoms. In Chapter 3 you made a list of your symptoms that you may wish to consult before proceeding. The table on the next page lists the symptoms that accompany the response to fear and the techniques outlined in this chapter that can be used to control them. Read through the list and identify how you react when you become fearful. Then put a check by the techniques you should master to handle your fear on the airplane.

Matching Coping Techniques to Your Symptoms

Symptom	*Techniques*
Thoughts	
Racing negative thoughts	Thought stopping
I'll die	
I'll suffocate	
I'll have a panic attack	
I'll be trapped	
I'll make a fool of myself	
Hypervigilant attention to details of the flight	Thought stopping
Superstitious thoughts (I must call Mom to be safe)	Thought stopping
Can't think (forget things)	Thought stopping + RED
Physical Symptoms	
Racing heart	Valsalva maneuver RED (breathing)
Tense muscles	Identify, tense, relax (ITR)
TMJ	Piranha
Shoulders/neck	Turtle
Legs	Ballerina
Chest	ITR
Stomache	ITR
Throat	ITR
Tapping feet	Ballerina
Awkwardness when moving about	Ballerina
Clenching teeth	Piranha
Upset stomach	RED
Sweaty palms	RED

Headache	Turtle + RED
Dizziness	RED
Dry mouth	RED
Repeated trips to lavatory	RED
Stammering	RED

If you have other symptoms, try to determine whether they are related to muscle tension. If they are, use the identify, tense, relax strategy to control them. If not, simply take control of your breathing using the RED technique.

After you have identified your symptoms and the strategies that you are going to use on the plane to deal with them, begin to use them in your everyday life to handle other stressors. Your thoughts about flying are automatic. Up to this point, you have been defenseless against them. Now you are arming yourself with ways to regain control of your thoughts and your body. Prepare for your next flight as though you were going to war. You are.

In Chapter 9 you will prepare your own flight plan. This plan will incorporate the techniques you have identified here as well as some other information about the airplane, pilots, and the air traffic control system. You will be armed with techniques to deal with your automatic thoughts as well as the facts about air travel. You will also begin to practice flying using self-guided imageries before you take on the real thing.

Avoiding Avoidance

A portion of the strategy that you must follow as you battle your fear of flying is avoiding avoidance. You "grow" your fear when you avoid flying, and this in turn makes it harder to fly the next time. To fully consider what happens when you avoid a flight, imagine yourself in the following situation: Your boss calls on Wednesday evening and tells you that you have been selected to represent the company in San Antonio, Texas on Friday. He has asked his secretary to arrange for the airline tickets and hotel reservations. He also tells you that you can pick up the tickets in his office on Thursday. Your immediate reaction is fearful thoughts and the physical symptoms begin. Then, on Thursday morning, your boss calls again and tells you that the meeting has been called off. What do you experience? An overwhelming feeling of relief! Your stomach is no longer tied in a knot. Your palms stop perspiring. The muscles in your back and shoulders relax, and you can concentrate on your work. Your body re-laxes, and your mind stops focusing on flying.

What happens when you make a reservation, go to the airport, and then fail to board the plane? The same feeling of relief, and perhaps the recurring thought that you just missed flying to your death. These feelings of relief are so powerful that they actually reinforce the negative thoughts and the avoidance of airplanes. What may be worse, after you avoid, you will probably criticize yourself unmercifully, which lowers your self-esteem and weakens your ability to confront your fear in the future. The result is that the more often you give into your fear, the more likely you will avoid flying.

After you have mastered the techniques outlined in this chapter, ac-quired the information in Chapters 5 and 6, and prepared your own flight plan, it will be time to make a reservation and fly. Do not plan to fly until you are reasonably sure that you will follow through with your plans. When you next make a reservation, you must be like the woman who put her arm through mine as we were approaching her graduation flight and said, "Duane, I'm going to the restroom and kiss myself goodbye, but I'm getting on that plane." She admitted to a reporter who covered the semi-nar for CNBC later that she was totally frightened when she boarded the plane the first time, but she did it! Her relaxed smile while on the return flight was a testimony to her victory.

Summary

Your mind responds automatically to the fearful stimulus: air travel. Your body reacts. If you are to be successful in your efforts to win the battle against your fear, you need to have strategies to deal with the mind and with the physical reaction to fear. Thought stopping, RED, the Valsalva maneuver, and relaxing tense muscles by identifying the muscle tension, increasing the tension, and cuing the relaxation can put you in control. Identify your symptoms and begin to practice today.

5

Developing a Valid Information Base: Personnel, Planes, and the Industry

You, like almost every fearful flyer, have been told that flying is the safest mode of transportation. The fact that you are still fearful means that you do not believe what you were told. You are skeptical for two reasons. One has to do with the way the human mind works: after we develop a belief, we take in information selectively. We listen more intently to information that supports what we already believe than we do to information that refutes what we believe. Second, you, along with everyone else, receive a great deal of misinformation about airplanes, the personnel associated with the industry, and the industry itself. We receive this misinformation from the media, from the people around us; even from people who should know better. More about this in a moment.

If you believe that flying is one of the most dangerous things you can do, does this mean that you will always have this belief? Not necessarily, but it does mean that you will have to work a great deal harder than most people to absorb objective information about air travel. It also means that you have to start evaluating the credibility of the information you receive. If you get on a plane and the flight attendants tell you, "We've been flying through thunderstorms all day," should you believe them? If you read in the most reputable newspaper in the country that there were hundreds of "near misses" in the skies across the country last year, should you believe that thousands of people on airplanes narrowly missed dying in midair collisions? If a reputable telejournalist reports that a Midwest Express jet crashed because someone installed bogus parts in the engines, and that the problem is widespread, should you believe that defective parts are about to bring dozens of planes crashing to the ground, killing thousands of unsuspecting people? If you are truly a fearful flyer, you will believe these reports, and those from less reputable sources that claim every airplane that takes off is likely to crash, killing everyone aboard.

Would you believe me if I told you that all of the events reported above actually happened, and they were all misrepresentations of the truth? They did, and they were. Flight attendants are taught nothing about flying, nor about the policies that govern pilots who fly planes. In fact, they know less about flying than you will after you read this book. Several fearful flyers have told me that flight attendants told them of flying directly through thunderstorms. As you will learn in Chapter 6 that could not have happened.

How Misinformation Is Spread

After a "thorough " investigation, CBS news reported that a Midwest Express DC-9 crashed after takeoff on September 6, 1985 because faulty parts had been installed in an engine. The National Transportation Safety Board (NTSB) reported that in fact "a compressor spacer in the right engine had failed," and further investigation revealed that the assembly was not an FAA (Federal Aviation Administration) approved part. CBS's story verified! Not quite. The NTSB reported that the crew made a mistake in dealing with the failed engine and this contributed immeasurably to the crash. This vital fact was not included in the CBS report. Neither was the fact that planes can fly quite nicely on one engine if the pilot makes the proper correction after an engine fails.

CBS news was trying to make the point that bogus parts were a problem throughout the industry. In fact, they were a problem for some airlines at the time of the report, but only for those airlines that subcontracted maintenance procedures to a few disreputable businesses. The problem was quickly identified and corrected by the FAA and the industry itself.

What should CBS news have reported? "A Midwest Express DC-9 crash resulted from the initial failure of an engine and an improper reaction by the crew." That would have been objective reporting, but that would not have corresponded with the story line that bogus parts are a major hazard to the flying public. No person has ever died in plane crash solely because of faulty parts. This story illustrates how the media distorts the news about air travel to fit their own purposes and scares an unsuspecting public in the process.

Reports of Near Misses

The "Near Miss" Story carried by many leading newspapers also illustrate how distorted information gets into "factual" stories in the media. This story actually surfaces from time to time, but, before you can evaluate it, you need some facts. Commercial planes flying below 29,000 feet are spaced 1,000 feet apart vertically and 3 to 20 miles apart in horizontally. Above 29,000 feet planes are spaced 2,000 feet apart vertically and about 10 miles or more apart horizontally. Every plane flying over the United States is being tracked by an air traffic controller on a radar screen and simultaneously monitored via radar by a computer. When planes deviate from these spacings, the computer automatically registers it as a near miss. Are planes 800 feet apart in danger of colliding? Certainly not. Are planes that are 2 miles apart in danger of having a midair crash? Pilots laugh at this idea, because they know the planes and passengers are in no danger.

I am not suggesting that there has never been a near miss. Occasionally, planes come within a few hundred feet of each other. Between 1982 and mid-1995 there were three midair crashes involving commercial air carriers. The number of people killed in these crashes is 103. This is less than the number of people killed on U.S. highways in one day. You should also know that pilots have tremendous incentive to stay on course. Because planes are on radar at all times, and thus monitored much as you are in your car when you pass through a highway patrol radar trap, a significant deviation from course results in an automatic fine for the pilot. These fines, which can reach $10,000, are paid by the pilot, not the airline.

Beyond the Headlines

The fact is, the media thrives on plane crashes and stories of near disaster because such stories attract readers and viewers. One telejournalist told me that the people in his newsroom cheered when they learned that the crash of a DC-10 in Sioux City, Iowa had been captured on videotape. As you have undoubtedly noticed, stories of airplane disasters are reported over and over again. This produces another type of misperception: planes crash all the time. Newspapers and television stations frequently carry stories about the crashes on the anniversary of the flights. Several of the more dramatic accidents have been made into movies, the most recent of which was about the aforementioned 1989 crash of the United DC-10 in Sioux City.

In 1994, which was one of the worst years in history for the airline industry, four planes crashed: two American Eagle commuters and two USAir jets. That is far too many, but that was four out of about 10 million flights that originated in this country in that year. I like the odds; particularly when you consider that on the average, over the last decade, less than 100 people have died per year in plane crashes. The total number of fatalities in the 1994 plane crashes exceeded 300. In less than seventy-two hours that many people die in automobiles.

The information presented in this chapter and the next was gathered over the past five years from the FAA, the NTSB, and from more than a dozen American Airlines pilots who have more than 200 years of flying experience among them. In this chapter I will answer fearful flyers' most frequently asked questions about pilots and other personnel associated with the flight, about planes, and about the airline industry, starting with the latter topic. In Chapter 6 I will answer the questions most frequently asked about flight planning, including preparing for bad weather, and turbulence. I do not attempt to portray flying as *perfectly safe*. It isn't. It is simply the safest and fastest way to get from point A to point B.

The Airline Industry

As a group, U.S. carriers are the safest in the world, followed closely by the Western European carriers and the Pacific Rim carriers. Why? Having safe air carriers requires government oversight, technological sophistication, competition for passengers, and the ability of companies to invest millions of dollars in training and equipment. When governments are unstable, or totalitarian, as they were in Russia and still are in China, government scrutiny may be missing. In countries that are poor or have unstable economies, the ability of companies to spend the money required, to purchase modern equipment or maintain older equipment, and to train pilots, mechanics, and other personnel involved with the flight is limited.

You are fortunate because you can get to almost any destination in the world on a safe airline. If you must take flights inside Russia, China,

India, and third-world countries, you will have to use airlines that have poor safety records. According to a study by Arnold Barnett and Mary Higgins, which you will read more about in a moment, your risk of being in a crash on airlines such as Aeroflot, Lot Polish, and Air India is about eight times as great as it is if you fly U.S. or Western European carriers. That probably makes those riskier airlines about as unsafe as driving to work on the New Jersey Turnpike or the Santa Ana freeway in Los Angeles. The answers to this first group of questions give you some insight into the magnitude of the industry and what safety means in terms of risks, airlines' records, and economics.

How many flights originate in the United States and Canada each year?

Few people are aware of the magnitude of the airline industry. Each year approximately ten million flights take off and land in this country. One and one-half million flights originate in Canada. One estimate by the FAA suggests that nearly 100,000 people are in the skies over the United States during the daylight hours day in and day out. If you believe the newspaper and the television reporters, you couldn't go outside for fear that a plane would fall on you.

Is air travel really safe?

Arnold Barnett of the Massachusetts Institute of Technology and Mary Higgins of the Air Force Center for Studies and Analyses studied the safety records of the U.S. domestic airlines from 1977 to 1986. Their major conclusions were that the domestic carriers are the safest in the world and that they were four times safer in the decade studied than they were in the early seventies. They also concluded that flying was ten times safer than it was in the early sixties. They estimated that the death rate risk per flight was one in eleven million (*Management Science*, January 1989). Air travel has become even safer since the Barnett/Higgins publication. The FAA at one time estimated that air travel is 200 times safer than automobile travel, but a more reasonable estimate is that it is 20 times safer.

Comparing Planes, Trains, and Automobiles

An Iowa State University statistician computed the probability of your dying in various ways. As already noted, the probability of a plane crashing when you are flying domestically is one in ten to eleven million. The probability when you are aboard an international flight is approximately one in four and one-half million. However, if you fly on the world's safest airlines and avoid commuters, these probabilities go up dramatically.

The probability that you will die in an automobile crash if you are an average driver is about one in five thousand. Most fearful flyers are under the illusion that they are "bullet proof" when they are driving because they feel as if they are in control. Each day, about 115 people die on U. S. highways. Approximately 50 percent of these fatalities involve drunk drivers who run into people who are in control of their car, but not in control of the drunk driver.

Trains are very safe, and many fearful flyers choose trains over planes. The probability of dying in a train accident is approximately 1 in 367,000 if you are the average train passenger. Fearful flyers feel as if they have some control on board a train because they can stop the train and get off. That's true, but trains are not as safe as flying on regularly scheduled airplanes.

Do all domestic airlines have the same safety records?

Between 1989 and 1994 USAir was averaging one crash per year according to FAA reports, while Southwest Airlines had yet to have a crash resulting in a fatality. In 1993 the International Airline Passengers Association identified five U.S. carriers as being among the world's safest airlines: American Airlines, Delta Airlines, Southwest Airlines, America West Airlines, and Alaska Airlines. This association also recommended Continental Airlines, Northwest Airlines, United Airlines, Trans World Airlines, and USAir (*San Francisco Chronicle*, 2 Sept. 1993). I wonder why USAir appeared on the recommended list given their record for the early nineties, although in 1995 the FAA commended USAir for its efforts to improve its safety record. On a personal note, I chose not to fly on USAir in the early nineties, but I would have no qualms about boarding one of their planes at this time.

Are commuter airlines as safe as the larger carriers?

Crashes involving fatalities occur about four times more frequently on commuters than they do on the large carriers, according to an article in the July 1991 issue of *Consumer Reports.* A more recent comparison of the safety records of regular airlines versus commuter airlines that appeared in *Newsweek,* 24 April 1995 also suggests that commuters are less safe than other airlines.

I view commuters as only slightly safer than the automobile. The article in *Consumer Reports* suggests that the safety records of commuters are improving, but I doubt if they will ever reach the safety records of the large jets. I fly commuters, but I feel much more secure on those commuters associated with the safest airlines listed under the previous question. The *Newsweek* article reports, "The typical commuter airline has a death risk of 1 in 1.5 million." The typical major airline has a death risk that is several times more favorable. Not flying on commuters, unlike not flying on large jets, will not severely limit your lifestyle. It will take you six to eight hours to drive to a destination that you could have flown to in one hour, however.

Is international flight as safe as flying domestically?

U.S carriers are among the safest in the world, so the answer to the question is no if you consider all foreign airlines as a group. However, there are many excellent and safe foreign carriers. Among those placed on the list of the world's safest airlines by the International Airline Passengers Association (*San Francisco Chronicle,* 2 Sept. 1993) were British Airways, Lufthansa, SAS, ANA (All Nippon Airways), Ansett Australia Airlines, Canadian Airlines, Saudi Arabian Airlines, Finnair, KLM, Malaysian Airlines, and Swissair. Japan Air Systems was placed on the group's recommended list. Ansett, Canadian Airlines, KLM, and Finnair have never had a fatality. Worldwide, including the United States, there are twenty-eight airlines that have never had a fatality, including Southwest, Air New Zealand, and America West.

Are there any unsafe airlines?

In July 1990 *Traveler* magazine published the safety records of the world's major airlines using the period from 1969 to 1988 as the basis for their analysis. The ten airlines with the worst records during that period, starting with the least safe airline, were Aeroflot (Russia), China, Egypt Air, Air India, Turkish Air, CAAC (China), Philippine Airlines, Korean Air, Lot Polish, and Avianca (Columbia).

How can I keep track of the safety records of various airlines?

Be aware that airlines are constantly striving to maintain high standards of safety. Airlines that are perceived as unsafe lose millions of dollars in business. You can keep up on the safety records of airlines by subscribing to magazines such as *Traveler* and *Consumer Reports,* which periodically publish articles about airline safety. You can also call the National Transportation Safety Board and ask about the safety record of an airline. They also maintain information about the safety of foreign airports.

What about the charter airlines? Are they safe?

It is difficult to get information about these airlines, but they fly under slightly different rules than do the regularly scheduled commercial carriers. Some of them have been cited for safety deficiencies. Here again, the best way to get information about the particular airline is to call the National Transportation Safety Board. However, if the charter plane is owned by one of the major carriers that has a good record, relax and enjoy your trip.

What factors other than safety should I consider when choosing an airline?

Research by airline companies suggests that the cost of the ticket is the primary basis people use for choosing an airline. However, because ticket prices and safety records are quite similar among the leading carriers, you may wish to consider the customer service record of the carrier. An article in the July 1991 issue of *Consumer Reports* gives satisfaction with service ratings of the major U.S. airlines. Alaska led the list with a satisfaction rating of 83. It was followed by Delta (76), America West (78), Southwest (74), and American (72). Subsequent, but less scientific, reports support the *Consumer Reports* survey results.

The service records of foreign carriers are not readily available, but generally speaking, European carriers get higher marks for service by the people with whom I have spoken than do U.S. carriers, and people rave about some of the Pacific Rim carriers, such as Malaysia Air.

Are the airlines that file for Chapter 11 (bankruptcy) cutting corners on safety?

Filing for Chapter 11 allows airlines to operate without having their creditors seize their assets. The idea that these airlines are unsafe probably started with reports, which were later verified, that Eastern Airlines' supervisors falsified repair records on some airplanes. It is probably worth reporting that when Eastern stopped flying they were among the top ten safest airlines in the world, and that no accidents occurred as a result of the falsified repair reports. But the idea that someone would falsify repair records is troublesome.

To assess the risk associated with being in Chapter 11, it is important that you understand what occurs when an airline files for protection against its creditors. First, the FAA sends additional air safety inspectors to monitor that company. Second, the airline's insurance companies become involved in providing oversight of the day-to-day operations of that carrier. This occurs because they want to ensure the safest possible operation.

Many airlines have been in Chapter 11, including Northwest, America West, Eastern, TWA, Pan Am, and Continental. Except for Eastern and Pan Am, which have ceased operations, these airlines are listed among the twenty safest airlines in the world. TWA has not had a fatality in the last ten years, according to *Newsweek* (29 April 1995). Of the major carriers, Northwest Airlines' safety record ranks second behind American Airlines, which is the safest major carrier in the world, according to the *Traveler* survey mentioned earlier.

I must confess that I do not like to fly on airlines that are financially troubled, but not because of safety. These airlines will repair their airplanes, but they may not repair their baggage-handling equipment. They will fly safely, but they may cancel flights if it will save them money. The result: poorer service and reduced on-time arrivals in many instances.

What is the international language of the airline industry?

All pilots and air traffic controllers must be able to speak English. This facilitates communication when U.S. airlines fly to other countries and when foreign carriers come to this country. If you are aboard an Iberian plane (the Spanish national airline) and it is flying to Spain, the crew and the air traffic controllers will speak in their native tongue, however. This will be true of any airliner traveling to its country of origin because this facilitates communication between the pilots and controllers.

Is safety good business?

USAir lost $40 million in bookings after it had two crashes in 1994, according to *Newsweek* (29 April 1995), and American Eagle estimated that it lost $20 million because of the events that resulted from two of its 1994 crashes. Other airlines have experienced similar results when their safety records came under scrutiny.

Millions of fearful flyers believe that the airline industry will cut corners and endanger their lives. This is flawed thinking. Consider that a crash may result in the loss of a plane worth $20 and $120 million. In addition, if the company has been negligent, the liability lawsuits can cost them many more millions. Then there are the advertising costs that will be incurred as the airline tries to rebuild its image as a safe carrier. Safety pays huge dividends.

Pilots and Pilot Training

Commercial airline pilots are carefully selected, trained, and supervised. The portrayal of them as daredevils willing to risk their lives and those of their passengers represents one of the most erroneous stereotypes imaginable. Many pilots have commented, "I am the first one to arrive at the scene of an accident." This means that when a plane crashes, the pilot is likely to die along with many of the passengers. Other pilots put it more graphically, "My butt is strapped to that plane just like the passengers. I have a life that I want to get back to." One pilot has a picture of his wife and four children taped inside his hat. When a nervous passenger asks if the flight is going to be a safe one, he simply shows the passenger the picture and indicates he wants to return to his family. Answers to the following questions should help you develop trust in the men and women who become pilots of U.S. carriers.

What is the background of the typical airline pilot?

It is important to note that airlines hire people who already know how to fly. The training that they receive after being hired focuses on how to fly commercial planes following FAA and company policies. Pilots come to the airlines from two sources: civilian and military. Currently, most commercial airline pilots start their careers in the military, but this is likely to change in the future because of the downsizing of the armed forces.

Military pilots typically attend one of the service academies (for example, the Air Force Academy) or complete a ROTC (Reserve Officers' Training Corps) program during their undergraduate training. After candidates for pilot training undergo a rigorous physical, they are selected for pilot training, and if they complete that training, they become military pilots. After completing their military obligation, most pilots have completed the training necessary to acquire an ATP (air transport pilot) license and have accumulated more than the minimum 1,500 hours needed to apply for a position at a major airline.

Pilots who pursue the civilian route to becoming a commercial airline pilot may attend one of the colleges or universities that offer an undergraduate training program focusing on airlines technology (for example, Florida Institute of Technology), or they may simply take advantage of the inexpensive flying lessons offered by many universities (for example, Purdue University). These pilots will acquire a number of licenses on their way to the ATP license, including a single-engine license, a multiengine license, and an instrument rating that allows them to fly on instrument flight rules (IFR) as opposed to flying visually (VFR). Civilian pilots may take a variety of jobs, such as teaching others to fly, flying cargo planes, flying corporate jets, and flying for commuter airlines, on their way to qualifying as a pilot for a major carrier. Ultimately, civilian and military pilots compete for jobs with the major airlines. While there has been some debate about which pilots are the best, the fact is that both routes produce good pilots.

What are the characteristics of these would-be pilots?

Most aspiring pilots are at least twenty-one years old, probably have a college education, and may have an advanced degree. They are mostly men, although more and more women are taking both the military and civilian routes and becoming pilots. They are typically in their late twenties and early thirties, in excellent health, have extremely stable personalities, and have accumulated more than 3,000 hours of flight time. There are no inexperienced pilots in the cockpits of the airplanes in this country.

What happens after someone applies for a job as an airline pilot?

The companies begin the screening process by running extensive background checks on each candidate to verify his or her credentials. Applicants are then screened in several ways. They are given an extensive battery of psychological tests to assess aptitude and stability. They must demonstrate their ability to fly in a simulator. A preliminary review of the candidate's family health history is also made. If there is a family history of heart disease or other debilitating illness, it is unlikely that the candidate will be hired. Finally, they are subjected to a rigorous interview by a panel of pilots, some of whom may be retired.

Once a preliminary decision has been made to hire the candidate, he or she is given a rigorous physical examination, which includes an EEG and an EKG. Drug testing is done at this time. When candidates pass the rigorous physical, they are hired and placed in training. It is also worth noting that when airlines are hiring, they have many applicants for every opening.

What is the nature of the initial training pilots receive?

Newly hired pilots enter the older, established companies such as United, American, and Delta in one of two positions: flight engineer or first officer. Newly hired pilots who are employed by Southwest, Midway, America West, and many of the newer carriers will enter the flying ranks as a first officer because these carriers do not fly planes with older technology.

Older airplanes such as the B-727 and the DC-10 have three-person crews: captain, first officer, and flight engineer. The captain is in charge of the crew, the airplane, and the cargo. The first officer, who alternates flying the plane with the captain, sits in the right seat in the cockpit (the captain is in the left seat). The flight engineer faces an instrument panel (some pilots call this riding side-saddle) and monitors several systems, including heating, air conditioning, and the hydraulics, which is the system that operates the landing gear and the control devices located on the wing and elsewhere. Newer planes, such as the DC-9-80, the F-100, and the B-767, are equipped with computers that perform the systems monitoring function and thus do not have a flight engineer.

Stages of Training

Pilot training is increasingly computer assisted: that is, teaching programs have been developed that contain the information pilots need. The computer "teaches" the lesson to the pilot and assesses whether he or she has learned the material that was presented by administering a computerized test. However, once the computer has completed its work, the pilot must undergo a rigorous oral examination administered by the FAA representative or company instructor who has been appointed by the FAA (called a *check airman* even if she is a woman) to verify that the knowledge has been acquired.

The final phase of the training takes place in the simulator. Simulators are exact replicas of the cockpit of the airplane that the new pilot will operate. They can simulate all aspects of flight, including takeoffs, landings, and emergencies, such as engine fires. In the simulators, new pilots must demonstrate that they can perform their jobs to the satisfaction of the FAA or an FAA-appointed simulator instructor (also called a check airman).

Unlike many other industries, airlines train new pilots to proficiency. This means that the pilots must demonstrate that they can handle every aspect of their job to the satisfaction of the instructors. After simulator training is complete, new pilots are assigned to the plane for which they were trained. For the first fifteen to twenty-five hours in their new positions, pilots are supervised by a company supervisor (a check airman) to make certain that they perform satisfactorily.

Newly hired pilots are placed on probationary status for one year at most airlines. At the end of each month, they are evaluated by the captain of the crew with which they have been flying. If these evaluations are satisfactory and the pilots maintain their proficiency, probationary status is removed after one year.

Do pilots have to return for training after they are hired?

No group of professionals has more continuing education than pilots. Some airlines require captains to return for recurrent training every six months, although the trend is to require recurrent training annually. During this recurrent training, pilots go to their company's training center (affectionately called the schoolhouse by many pilots) for intensive training regarding all aspects of their job. Flight engineers and first officers also return to their training centers for recurrent training once per year.

During these training periods the pilots (captains and first officers) must demonstrate that they are proficient in all aspects of flying the plane. Flight engineers must demonstrate their ability to operate the control panel. During recurrent training, all crew members are updated on any new developments in the industry, but more importantly, they are checked to see how they function in the case of abnormal or emergency situations. Because emergency situations are so rare in airplanes, recurrent training is the only way that pilots can maintain their ability to deal with them.

If pilots or flight engineers fail to demonstrate that they can perform either routine or emergency procedures, their training will be continued until they can do so. If they cannot perform satisfactorily, they are dismissed from the airline. The bottom line is that all the people who fly commercial airplanes must put their job on the line at least once a year. Do any of them fail recurrent training? Not very many, because they are so carefully selected at the start; but a few do, and they are dismissed.

How does a flight engineer or first officer get to be a captain?

The answer to this question is quite simple: seniority. Airline captains must retire at age sixty. This creates opportunities for pilots to advance, first from flight engineer to first officer, then from first officer to captain. As you might imagine, one of the reasons crew members want to advance is pay. Captains make more money than first officers, who in turn make more money than flight engineers.

Once a crew member qualifies by virtue of seniority to advance, he or she must go back for what is termed upgrade training. This lasts for varying lengths of time depending on whether the person is upgrading to a different airplane or is simply switching to another position on the same plane.

Are pilots qualified to fly more than one plane?

Because the cockpits of airplanes vary, a decision was made to restrict pilots to flying one plane to enhance safety. However, there is at least one exception to this rule. The cockpits of the Boeing 757 and 767 are identical. Pilots who qualify to fly one of these planes are qualified to fly both.

If there are two or three members in a crew, how is their work coordinated?

I have already mentioned that the captain is in charge of all aspects of the flight. This does not mean that he or she can ignore the input of others. Several years ago a plane landed in the wrong city. Although no one was hurt, there was a thorough investigation. It was learned that the first officer knew they were landing in the wrong place, but had been ordered to keep his mouth shut by a dictatorial captain. This and other incidents convinced the FAA and the airlines that they needed to alter the way the cockpit crews functioned.

All U.S. airlines have adopted a training program called Crew Resource Management, which has become an industry standard. This training teaches captains how to involve their crews in the decision-making process.

What about pilots' health? I worry that they will get sick during the flight.

The rules regarding physical checkups are the same as they are for recurrent training: captains must have complete physicals twice per year, first officers and flight engineers once per year. After forty pilots' physicals must include an EKG. In order to eliminate the possibility that a friendly family physician might not report the results of the physicals accurately, these examinations are administered by an FAA-appointed doctor. The results of the EKGs are transmitted directly via telephone to Oklahoma City, Oklahoma where they are interpreted by an FAA physician.

An additional safeguard: the airlines go so far as to specify that, when the pilots are eating during a flight, the captain and first officer are to be served different meals on the off chance that one of the meals should result in illness.

Does the use of drugs and alcohol by pilots endanger the flying public?

Drugs and alcohol are two separate issues with the same implication: pilots who use them would be impaired and could not operate the plane safely. However, drugs are illegal and, if pilots are caught using them, they are dismissed immediately. As noted earlier, one part of the screening process for new pilots is a drug test. If applicants fail the test, they are not hired. After hiring, pilots are subject to random drug testing and testing "for cause." For example, pilots involved in accidents are tested routinely.

Here are the steps in random drug testing:

1. A computer randomly selects employees to be tested.

2. An official from the airline meets the incoming plane, informs the pilots that they are to be tested, and specifies when and where the testing is to occur.

3. The pilots show up at the appointed place and provide urine samples.

4. The specimen is divided into two samples so that a second test can be run if the first is positive.

5. The samples are sent to a laboratory for testing.

If the sample is positive, the pilot can appeal. For example, early in the drug testing program, a pilot who had eaten poppy-seed rolls on his flight tested positive. Eating poppy seeds or drinking certain herbal teas produces what are termed *false positives*. Another pilot who had been injected with a morphine-based anesthetic in his visit to the dentist also tested positive. Both were cleared of drug usage. However, if pilots test positive for drug use, their flying career is terminated. How many pilots have tested positive? American Airlines, which has nearly ten thousand pilots, has never had a single positive test. Other airlines report similar results. Most pilots say that illegal drugs are not a problem in the cockpit. Based on everything I have learned, I concur with that assessment.

You may also be interested to know that there are severe restrictions on the legal drugs pilots may take and still fly. They cannot fly when taking drugs prescribed by a physician that contain barbiturates, codeine, and other similar substances. There are even restrictions on the over-the-counter drugs that a pilot may take and operate an airplane.

Alcohol Use

What about alcohol abuse? A highly publicized case in 1990 involved three members of a Northwest crew who were drinking the night before they flew from Fargo, North Dakota to Minneapolis led to additional scrutiny in this area. Ultimately, a random alcohol testing program was adopted, which began in January 1995.

The FAA rule is that pilots may not drink eight hours before a flight, and many airlines have stricter policies. For example, some airlines prohibit pilots from drinking twenty-four hours before a flight and while they are on *layover*. Pilots flying domestically fly what are termed multiple day trips. After several hours of flying, the FAA requires that pilots be permitted to rest. This typically occurs in a city other than the one in which the pilot is based. This is a layover. Pilots flying internationally fly from their bases to foreign destinations such as London or Tokyo and then "lay over" to rest before flying back to their bases in this country.

I examined the NTSB accident reports beginning in 1982. No accident has been attributed to alcohol use in the period from 1982 to 1995.

But what about those Northwest pilots? No accident occurred because of their consumption of alcohol. They were drinking a few hours before their flight and thus violated the FAA eight-hour rule and their company's rule of not drinking twelve hours before a flight. They were reported by a patron in the bar where they were drinking, met by federal officials at the conclusion of their flight, arrested, and subsequently tried, found guilty of breaking a federal law, fined, and sent to prison. Moreover, their licenses to fly were suspended and their careers terminated. Because captains flying for major airlines make from $75,000 to $200,000 per year, the drinks these pilots had were among the most expensive in history if you consider the loss of income, fines and lawyers' fees. Most pilots won't even go into a bar dressed in their uniforms and fastidiously avoided breaking the rules, even before the advent of random alcohol testing.

Up until January 1995 the airlines depended on self-monitoring and crew monitoring to control alcohol abuse in the industry, and these are still important safeguards against drinking on the job. Self-monitoring means that pilots were expected to monitor their own behavior and seek help if they began to abuse alcohol to the point that it influenced their functioning in the cockpit. Crews are also charged with monitoring each other. If a captain, first officer, or flight engineer knowingly flies with a person who is drinking, they can, and in all probability will, be dismissed from their jobs along with the offending crew member. A flight attendant who knows that one of the pilots has been violating the rules is also obligated to report that person. In addition, the FAA and some airlines operate what is sometimes referred to as 1-800-SNITCH lines, which can be used by crew or members of the public to report pilots who violate either the drug or alcohol use regulations.

Are pilots supervised on the job?

As already stated, the captain is in charge of the crew and has oversight responsibilities. However, captains and crew are given no-notice line checks, both by the FAA and company supervisors. The way this works is that the person who is going to perform the line check simply shows up, shows the captain his or her credentials, and states, "I will be flying with you today."

During this line check, the functioning of each crew member is checked, along with how the crew works together. Feedback about their functioning is provided at the end of the flight. In the unlikely event that some unusually bad practice is observed, the check airman has the prerogative of sending one or more crew members back to their company's training center for additional training. Every captain must have at least one line check each year or his or her license is suspended until the check can be scheduled.

What about stress? I understand that many pilots are overworked and that flying a plane is a high-stress occupation.

Research has shown that certain parts of flying are quite stressful, particularly those parts of the flight involving takeoff and landing. In order to reduce this load, the captain and the first officer alternate flying various segments or "legs" of the flight. However, the stress experienced by pilots is not due to danger, but is related to the workload during takeoffs and landings.

When you are considering the stress an airline pilot must endure, it may be useful to know that the FAA restricts pilots to flying 100 hours per month, and union contracts often restrict the number of hours flown to as little as 75 hours per month. The amount of flying time is measured in minutes from the time the plane pushes back from the jet bridge to its return to the jet bridge. The time that pilots spend waiting for passengers to board is not counted as flight time, only that time when they are actually operating the aircraft. The result is that in some instances pilots put in very long days, and while the FAA requires that they be given adequate time to rest before they fly again, the job can be quite tiring. Pilots who make transcontinental and transoceanic flights are also dealing with the stressors associated with adjusting to different time zones.

Pilots for major airlines have a stressful job, but generally speaking, this is probably compensated for by relatively short work weeks. On the other hand, pilots for many of the commuter airlines fly the maximum amount of time allowed by law and make many takeoffs and landings during the time they are flying. There is growing concern that stress and fatigue may represent major problems among these pilots. The FAA is currently considering revising the rules that govern commuter pilots' working conditions.

What about pilots on transoceanic flights? Don't they get tired? I've even heard stories that they sometimes go to sleep.

The airline industry is aware that fatigue can be a major problem on long flights. For this reason they put an extra pilot on flights to Europe and an extra crew on longer flights to places such as Tokyo. In addition, seats in the passenger cabin are reserved for the crew so they can rest, and on some planes, such as the MD-11 (McDonnell Douglas) and the Boeing-built B-747-400, bunks are provided.

In spite of these efforts, there have been documented cases of crew members going to sleep on long flights. The FAA is now considering letting crew members take catnaps during long flights to keep them refreshed.

Should you worry about the crew sleeping? Not for a second. There has never been an accident involving a U.S. carrier that was due to the crew sleeping. The fact is that the plane is on autopilot for most of these long flights anyway, and the crew's chief responsibility is to monitor the autopilot.

Do pilots think they are in a dangerous occupation?

In the September 1993 issue of *Traveler* magazine, Gary Stoller reported the results of a survey of commercial airline pilots. Forty-five percent of the pilots responding thought that flying was as safe in 1993 as it was in 1983. Another 35 percent thought that flying was just as safe in 1993 as it was in 1983. Some 20 percent of the pilots surveyed believed that flying was less safe in 1993 than it was in 1983.

I have yet to meet an airline captain who thinks that he or she is in an unsafe occupation. No one in Stoller's sample suggests that a pilot's job is hazardous either. If Barnett and Higgins's statistics on safety records covered earlier are correct, you could board a plane each day for the next thirty thousand years before you would be in a plane crash. Then you have a 60 percent chance of survival!

Personnel Other Than Pilots

The airline industry is staffed by carefully selected, highly trained professionals who are regularly supervised and retrained. Everyone connected with the flight is randomly drug tested, and mechanics, like pilots, must have a license issued by the FAA. There is room for improvement, and I suggest that you get the facts and write to your representatives and senators and urge them to make airline safety a high priority. This group of questions and answers provides information on mechanics, flight attendants, and air traffic controllers.

How are mechanics trained and supervised?

The training and selection of mechanics is similar to that of pilots. They come to the airlines after being trained in the military or attending an FAA-approved civilian school. They often start with smaller airlines and work their way up to major airlines. They are drug tested just as pilots are, and their work is subject to the same level of scrutiny. For example, after a repair is completed on an airplane, the mechanic who made the repair signs the plane's log book and places his or her employee number beside the signature. Then a supervisor checks that the repair has been made properly and also signs the log book and places his or her employee number beside the signature. If that repair fails, the mechanic and the supervisor are subject to fines as large as $5,000, and there is no guesswork about who was responsible.

In order to keep up-to-date and maintain their skills, mechanics undergo rigorous recurrent training on an annual basis. You should also be aware that the FAA provides oversight for mechanics and the repair process.

What is the function of flight attendants?

It is surprising to most people to learn that the primary job of flight attendants is to ensure the safety of the passengers. If you have flown, you know that they read a set of safety instructions regarding seat belts, flotation devices, and the use of oxygen masks before each flight. You also know that they check to be sure that passengers have their seat belts fastened before each flight and that the trays in the backs of each seat are in the upright position. You may not be aware that the announcement, "Flight attendants, prepare for departure," is a signal for the flight attendants to arm the emergency slides so that, in case of emergency, the slides will deploy and passengers can be evacuated safely.

It is even less likely that you know that flight attendants are trained in first aid, but that they are precluded from using the equipment and medication that is on board every flight. However, in the event of a medical emergency, one of the flight attendants will ask if there are medical personnel on board who can assist with the emergency. If this fails, the flight attendant will inform the captain that a medical emergency exists and the captain will land the plane at the first available site where the passenger can get assistance.

Finally, by now you have probably guessed that flight attendants' training focuses more on safety than it does on providing service. For example, flight attendants must demonstrate that they can evacuate a plane in ninety seconds with half the exits blocked. They also return for recurrent training once per year—training that focuses on safety. People who have been in emergency evacuations report that the flight attendants work well under the pressure of evacuating a plane.

How are flight attendants supervised?

FAA and company representatives observe flight attendants without their knowledge. Individuals or crews that function improperly can be fined or dismissed.

Are air traffic controllers competent?

In the 1980s, when Ronald Reagan was president, he fired the striking air traffic controllers. Supervisors and replacements from the military were brought in to substitute for the controllers who had been fired. This led to a persistent and reoccurring rumor that air traffic controllers are incompetent, and thus there is increased danger of midair collisions.

Your chances of being struck by space junk returning to earth is probably greater than your chances of being in a midair collision. However, it is important for you to know that the current air traffic controllers are well trained and supervised and that many of the problems, (such as job stress), that brought about the strike during the Reagan era have been resolved. I suggest that you visit a control tower near you to see these people in action. It will be very reassuring.

One of the major safety advances since the Reagan era has been the determination of the number of airplanes that can be safely handled at a particular destination. Once the airways approaching an airport are "saturated"—that is, filled with all the planes that can be handled safely—no more planes are allowed into that airspace. For the most part, this means that delays are now waited out on the ground instead of in holding patterns around the airport. This is safer and more economical because of the fuel needed in holding patterns. But what happens if a thunderstorm develops and the airport at your destination is closed after your plane is en route? The captain may be asked to slow the speed of the aircraft, fly vectors (fly a zigzag path), or be placed in a holding pattern for a short period of time. All of these maneuvers are perfectly safe. And yes, they have enough fuel to vector or hold, a topic to be addressed in greater detail in Chapter 6. The most important point: air traffic controllers do not accept more planes into their air space than they can safely handle.

I have heard that air traffic controllers do
not have the most up-to-date equipment
available to them. Is this true?

It is true that controllers do not always have the most up-to-date equipment. The FAA has been slow to require that equipment such as computers and radar systems be updated. One result of this is that there are more delays than would be the case if the best equipment was available. In one case, which will be discussed in the next chapter, an accident involving wind shear might have been avoided if Doppler radar had been installed at the Charlotte, North Carolina airport.

Questions About Airplanes

The modern airplane is a technological marvel. One of the reasons that the safety of air travel has increased over the past twenty-five years is the increased sophistication of the planes. Redundancy in critical parts such as altimeters and navigational equipment, as well as entire systems, and the development of specialized safety equipment are the primary reasons that accidents caused by mechanical problems are increasingly rare.

I know that some of the airplanes being
flown by the airlines are thirty years old.
Aren't they dangerous?

This is the number one question about airplanes asked by fearful flyers, and the answer is a resounding no! Most fearful flyers think of airplanes as they do their cars. Automobiles wear out after so many years and miles. So do airplanes, but there is one significant difference: the airlines engage in preventive maintenance on an ongoing basis and completely overhaul airplanes on a regular schedule based on flight time or every four to five years. The modern jetliner receives eleven hours of maintenance work for each hour it is flying. Commuter planes, which are smaller, receive six hours of maintenance work for each hour they fly.

I visited the American Airlines facility in Tulsa, Oklahoma to view the renovation of the airplanes firsthand. This facility can handle as many as thirty-six jetliners at one time. In the first building I visited a DC-10, which can carry about 300 people. The landing gear had been removed, as had all the engines, many of the control devices on the wings, and the interior of the plane. Each part is inspected and brought back to new specifications. For example, engine parts, which are subjected to great heat and begin to deteriorate, are heat-treated to restore the molecular structure of the metal in the parts. They are then rebuilt piece by piece and painstakingly tested. At the end of this process, a crew flight-tests the plane and checks to determine whether it is operating properly. Then it is placed back in service as, essentially, a new plane. The price tag for this process: $1 million or more.

I also learned that oil samples are taken regularly from the engines of each plane and analyzed to determine whether they contain telltale ingredients that indicate the engine is about to fail. More impressive yet, the functioning of the engines of some planes is monitored by computer as they fly, and the data is analyzed to determine whether the engine is functioning normally. If there are any signs that an engine is not functioning properly, it is removed prior to failure.

Tire wear and pressure is checked routinely before each flight. So are all systems and instruments on the airplane. In order for the captain to fly a plane, all parts on the minimum equipment list must be in working order. If you experience a delay because of a mechanical problem, it is because a part is not functioning properly.

I have heard that planes have a lot of backup systems so that if one fails another is available. Is this true?

Redundancy is the watchword when airplanes are built. They are equipped with spare altimeters, compasses, weather radars, hydraulic pumps that operate the control devices, at least two systems that can be used to lower the landing gear, etc., etc. Also, planes have at least twice as much power as they need to fly. Thus if an engine fails at the most critical time in the flight, the plane can fly quite nicely on one engine on a two-engine plane, two engines on a three-engine plane, and three engines on a four-engine plane.

Are the manufacturers of airplanes regulated?

The FAA provides standards that must be met in the building of airplanes and inspectors who ensure that the standards are met. However, airplane manufacturers routinely exceed FAA standards in the manufacturing process. For example, the FAA requires that airplanes used in commercial air travel remain airworthy even if a hole develops in the plane.

In the past, many planes have continued to fly and have landed with rather large holes in them.

The FAA also requires that the wings of an airplane support at least one and one-half times the weight of the plane, but aircraft manufacturers exceed that recommendation. A fully loaded B-747-400 may weigh nearly a million pounds on takeoff if it is fully loaded with fuel. The wings on that plane will support in excess of two million pounds. Other planes are built to similar specifications.

Are some planes safer than others?

There is widespread belief that some planes are safer than others, even among some pilots. In the September 1993 article in *Traveler* magazine by Gary Stroller mentioned earlier, he reports that pilots believe the Boeing-built B-727 and B-757 are the safest narrow body (one aisle) planes and B-747 is the safest wide body (two aisles) plane. The Airbus 320, which is built by a European consortium in Toulouse, France, was viewed as the least safe narrow body plane and the DC-10 as the least safe wide body plane. Do the objective data support these observations? No! Stoller surveyed U.S. pilots, many of whom do not fly the planes they were rating. Stoller also reports that the DC-10 has undergone numerous changes to make it safe since the 1970s and that Northwest Airlines pilots who fly the A-320 love it.

It is the case that one commuter plane, the ATR-72 has come under scrutiny of late because of an American Eagle crash in 1994. It was determined that the plane and its predecessor, the ATR-42, which is also used by commuter airlines, have trouble when icing conditions exist, and the 1994 crash was attributed largely to the failure of the deicing system. American Airlines took immediate action when they learned of the problem with the ATR-72: they moved all of the planes to geographic areas where icing would not be a problem. This is a typical response when a problem is diagnosed, and in the case of the ATR-72, the problem has been remedied.

Do planes have specialized safety equipment?

Here is only partial list of the specialized safety equipment on planes:

- Ground warning alert proximity system: This system has been installed on all jetliners that fly in this country and is being installed on all commuter airplanes that do not currently have it.

Its function is to warn the pilot if the plane is coming dangerously close to the ground. It does this via a female voice that says, "Pull up, pull up."

- Wind shear detection devices: This system warns the pilot if the plane is in a dangerous weather condition called wind shear. Again, a voice comes on and says, "Wind shear, wind shear." This is the signal for the pilot to take evasive action.

- Traffic and collision avoidance system (TCAS): This system has been installed on all jetliners. Its purpose is to back up the air traffic control system and avoid midair collisions. It monitors other airplanes in the vicinity of the plane, and if a collision is imminent, gives the pilot directions on how to avoid it.

- Weather radar: The crew has access to weather information from several sources, including their own radar. They are taught to interpret radar so that they can avoid thunderstorms and other dangerous weather conditions.

Summary

The U.S airline industry is the finest and safest in the world, although there are excellent airline companies throughout the world. These companies are staffed by carefully trained and supervised personnel. It is demonstrably true that this industry has provided the flying public with the safest means of transportation. Because the industry is not perfect, accidents do happen. Some accidents that occur are preventable, and the FAA, the NTSB, and the airline industry are striving to eliminate them. Fearful flyers often want a guarantee that planes are safe. This is an impossible expectation. Flying will never be perfectly safe, but of course, none of life's activities are perfectly safe.

6

Developing a Valid Information Base: Aerodynamics, Flight Planning, Weather, Terrorism, and Miscellaneous Concerns

This chapter picks up where Chapter 5 left off—that is, providing you with a valid information base about flying. Please remember that I am not trying to demonstrate that flying is perfectly safe, only that it is the safest form of travel available to you. I am also trying to provide you with a factual information base so that you can interpret the things that happen to you on an airplane. This chapter discusses aerodynamics (what makes planes fly), flight planning, weather—a huge barrier to flying for many people—as well as some miscellaneous issues that fearful flyers often ask about.

Before I start answering questions again let me demonstrate how the media gives you misinformation under the guise of objective reporting.

In an article on 24 April 1995, the reporters at *Newsweek* were trying to make the point that the U.S. airline industry is losing ground in the safety supremacy race to Western European carriers. To make their point, they compared U.S. carriers to twenty international carriers, which is like comparing apples and oranges. I could select twenty international carriers that would include Aeroflot, Avianca, both major Chinese carriers, and a few others and "prove" that your death risk is extraordinarily higher on a foreign carrier than it is on U.S. carriers. My point: *Newsweek* juggled their figures to make their case. If the article that appeared in *Newsweek* had been submitted to a scholarly panel they would have laughed out loud.

Aerodynamics

Planes, like all other objects on this earth, are subject to natural laws, such as the laws of gravity and lift. One of the best ways to get over the feeling that planes are going to drop out of the sky at any moment is to understand the natrual forces that are used to get them into the air, to keep them there when they are flying, and yes, bring them down safely in emergency situations.

> *How can anything as large as an airplane*
> *stay in the air? It seems unnatural.*

Planes have four forces at work on them as they fly: (1) drag, due to wind resistance; (2) thrust, which comes from jet engines or propellers; (3) gravity; and (4) lift, which comes from the action of the wings. An airplane will fly if it has a large enough wing that can be pushed through the air fast enough by its engines so that it can overcome the forces of drag and gravity. As one pilot of thirty years put it, "Give me big enough wings and engines and I will fly the Empire State Building to London." However, for our discussion, you need a little more information than this.

Principle of the Pressure Wave

Thrust from a jet engine is produced because the engine ingests air through the front of the engine; compresses it; heats it, which causes it to expand; and then expels it through the rear of the airplane. This is not unlike what happens when you blow up a balloon and then release it in the air. Propellers, which are driven by jet engines on commuter planes, also produce thrust. The wing produces the lift needed to literally raise the plane off the ground by developing what is termed a *pressure wave*. A pressure wave, which is a condensed column of air, is created when a wing is pushed through the air at high speed at a certain angle of attack. This is similar to what happens when you fly a kite. The pressure wave travels with the plane as it passes through the air and always stands between the plane and the ground. As the plane moves faster, pressure wave intensifies, and the plane is lifted higher and higher.

Speed increases the size of the pressure wave. So does the size of the wing being pushed through the air. When the plane reaches the desired altitude, the pilot makes adjustments in the speed and/or the angle of attack of the wing, and the plane levels off. When pilots wish to descend, they can slow the speed by pulling the throttles back to idle and reduce the pressure wave. One pilot I worked with always told the fearful flyers in our classes to imagine their planes riding on solid columns of air. It may also help you to imagine this because that is virtually what happens.

Flaps and Slats

Airplane manufactures take advantage of the principle of the pressure wave to develop wings so that very large airplanes can fly at relatively low speeds. Remember, lift results from a wing being pushed through the air, and the resulting pressure wave is determined by speed, the size of the wing, and the angle at which the wing passes through the air. Manufacturers influence the intensity of the pressure wave by placing devices on the wings that can increase the size of the wing as well as the angle of attack. These devices are called *flaps* if they are located on the trailing edge of the wing. Some airplanes have movable devices on the front of wings known as *slats*. If you have flown, you have probably observed these parts on the wing move as the pilot prepares for takeoff, and again during the landing approach.

Takeoff speed for many planes is at about 150 miles per hour. The curvature of the wing is increased so the plane will be able to "lift off" at this speed. As soon as the plane gets into the air, it accelerates, and the curvature of the wing can be reduced. This is done by retracting the devices (flaps and slats) on the wings. Ultimately, these devices are retracted altogether because the wing can produce enough lift to keep the plane in the air without them. Lift increases geometrically with speed, which means that a wing will produce four times as much lift at 200 miles an hour as it will at 100 miles an hour. Once the slats and flaps are retracted, the wing produces plenty of lift to keep the plane in the air.

What if an engine fails just as we lift off?
Will we still have enough thrust to push the
plane through the air?

In Chapter 5 I covered the issue of how planes are built. I said that one of the FAA requirements for commercial airplanes is that two engine planes must be able to fly on one engine if one engine fails at the most critical portion of the flight. This provision includes takeoffs. Therefore, if an engine fails just as the pilot begins the liftoff, the plane will still fly safely. In recent history, both Delta and USAir planes have had engines drop off during takeoff with no adverse consequences.

If an engine fails, the pilot will return to the airport and land as quickly as possible to maximize your safety. You are in no danger during this return to the airport.

What if both engines fail on takeoff?

If both engines fail, the plane is going to come down. The odds of both engines failing on takeoff are in the trillions, however. In recent history (the last fifteen years), there has been one incident in which both engines failed on takeoff. An SAS Airlines plane crashed because large quantities of ice were ingested on takeoff due to improper deicing. Under current deicing regulations, that could not occur in this country. I'll address this topic more fully later in this chapter.

What would happen if both engines fail when
the plane has reached its cruising altitude?

Many fearful flyers, particularly those who are afraid of heights, worry about the plane falling out of the sky because of engine failure, turbulence, or wings coming off. These things do not happen, but let me answer the question with a question. How many engines does the space shuttle use when it returns to earth? The answer is none. It glides back to earth and lands with no engines. Commercial airliners are much better gliders than the space shuttle. They have a glide ratio of about fifteen to one, which means that for every foot they are in the air they can glide fifteen feet. Remember the SAS Airlines plane that crashed because the engines ingested ice? As Paul Harvey says, "Now I'm going to tell you the rest of the story." All of the people on board that plane survived the crash. The engine failures occurred at about 3,500 feet. The pilot was able to maneuver the plane and land in an open field. The newspapers called this crash a Christmas miracle. Like most modern day "miracles" the plane's landing was due to the skill of the pilot, the fact that airplanes do glide, and yes, a great deal of luck.

A plane flying at 35,000 feet can glide 525,000 feet (99.43 miles) if both engines fail. In many parts of the United States there would be a landing strip available to the pilot. If you fly up and down the East Coast, get a window seat and make an X on a napkin every time you pass over an airport or the pilot makes an announcement that you have just passed over a city that has an airport. In other parts of the United States, the plane could be landed on a super highway, which is illegal. However, I have been told by more than one pilot that, given the choice between being fired and a crash, the pilot will take the former. Translation: the modern airline pilot wants to survive as much as you do and will land on a super highway if no other alternatives are available and that option presents itself.

What if we are flying over water and the plane has to land because of engine failure? Will the plane float?

Fearful flyers leave no stone unturned when thinking about the problems that can befall them on airplanes. *Ditching* is the term used to describe landing an airplane on a lake or in the ocean. No U.S. commercial jetliner has ever ditched, so very little is known about what will happen. Modern jetliners will float if placed in a swimming pool or landed in a lake or in the ocean, so long as they remain intact. Once a military jet was forced to land in the Pacific. It not only held together, it floated so well the military had to shoot holes in it to sink it, because it was in the shipping lanes and there was concern that a boat might hit it. Again, the probability that your plane will land in the water is very, very remote.

I do want you to know that planes that fly over water are equipped with flotation devices and that flight attendants are trained to make water evacuations. However, I don't wear swimming trunks under my clothes when I fly to Europe or the Caribbean, and I will not recommend the practice to you.

I've heard the word stall. Doesn't that mean that the plane is going too slow and is about to fall out of the sky?

A stall does occur when the wings of the plane are not moving fast enough through the air to produce the lift needed to keep it in the air. It should be comforting to know that pilots are as concerned about stall as you are, and devices in the cockpit monitor the speed of the aircraft to make sure that stalls do not occur. As a result, pilots are very conservative in computing the air speed needed to keep the plane flying at times in the flight other than touchdown. For example, prior to each takeoff pilots compute the speed needed to lift the plane safely off the runway. This computation is based on the weight of the aircraft, cargo, and passengers, as well as weather conditions. In this computation, and all others regarding flying speed, pilots use a safety margin of 30 percent. If the plane will lift off at 120 miles per hour, they set the takeoff speed at 156 miles per hour.

What is the most dangerous part of the flight?

Pilots have a quick answer to this question, the trip to the airport. Most fearful flyers have another answer, the takeoff. They are certain that this is the most dangerous part of the flight. Conversely, they love landings because they will be back on terra firma and safe from the dangers of flying. Actually, the landing is the most dangerous part of the flight, but it is not as dangerous as walking across the street, eating a hot dog, climbing a ladder, or shopping in a large mall—things people who are afraid to fly do every day. Pilots perform safe landings thousands of times per day all over the world. One airline, USAir, will have 5,000 takeoffs and landings today, tomorrow, the next day, and so forth. The landing is a highly controlled maneuver and so is the takeoff.

Flight Planning and the Flight Itself

Flight planning, like all aspects of the airline industry, is conducted with safety in mind. Everything, including fuel planning and route selection, is done with safety as the first priority. Moreover, flight planning is another example of how the FAA, the pilot, and the dispatcher serve as checks and balances to ensure safety. The FAA establishes the rules, the dispatcher develops an initial flight plan, and the captain examines the plan and approves it. Finally, the idea that flight planning is in any way haphazard should be banished from your mind. Nothing could be further from the reality of the situation.

Who plans the flights I take? It all seems so chaotic.

Flight planning is conducted initially by a person called a *dispatcher.* The dispatcher's job is to check weather reports as well as reports of turbulence and select a route for the flight. The dispatcher also checks the load (projected weight of the plane) and determines the fuel required for the flight. Ultimately, the dispatcher develops a flight plan that contains weather information; an estimate of the turbulence en route; the weight of the aircraft, including the fuel; and anything unusual about the airports from which the plane is departing or landing, such as runways that are closed. The flight plan also includes information about alternate airports, if any. Each flight must have an alternate airport if (1) there is the possibility of bad weather that might delay landing or close the airport altogether or (2) the airport to which the flight is going has only one runway. In some instances, a flight will be assigned a second alternate if there is a chance the first alternate would be unavailable because of weather. Once the dispatcher develops a flight plan, it is fed into the FAA computers so Air Traffic Control (ATC) can approve it. This allows ATC to regulate the flow of traffic taking off and landing at various airports, as well as the traffic on the various air routes.

Approximately thirty minutes before the flight, the captain prints out the flight plan and reviews it. If the information is not to his or her liking (for example, not enough fuel), changes can be requested. Ultimately, both the dispatcher, the captain, and ATC must agree on the information on the flight plan before the flight can be declared legal. Once the captain agrees with the flight plan, he or she signs it to signify acceptance. As you will see later, the flight plan is flexible and can be changed if bad weather develops en route.

Are there rules that govern flight plan development?

A list of these rules for flight plans follows:

1. A flight cannot be dispatched into areas of heavy turbulence.

2. A flight cannot be dispatched into a thunderstorm.

3. In order to be legal, a domestic flight must have enough fuel on board to fly to its destination and land. However, in determining the fuel load, many factors are considered. First, the weight of the airplane is calculated because the heavier the plane the more fuel required. Second, the weather en route and at the destination are considered. Since planes are not allowed to fly through thunderstorms, if one or more are likely during the flight, additional fuel is placed on board so the pilot can fly around the storms. If bad weather is possible at the destination, one or more alternate air-

ports must be chosen in case the plane cannot land at its destination. In this situation the plane must have enough fuel on board to go to the primary destination, travel to the most distant destination, hold for forty-five minutes, make a missed approach, and then make an approach and land.

Planes flying international routes have enough fuel on board to fly to their destination, make a missed approach to land, fly to their most distant alternate, hold for thirty minutes and land with 10 percent of their en route fuel still in their tanks.

4. A plane cannot be legally dispatched unless all equipment on the minimum equipment list is functioning.

5. When flying easterly headings, planes at cruising altitudes fly at odd-numbered altitudes (for example, 35,000; 37,000; 39,000). When flying in a westerly direction, planes must fly at even altitudes (for example, 24,000; 26,000).

I worry about the plane running out of fuel, particularly when we have delays. Is this a realistic worry?

Step 3 of the preceding answer is the best answer to this question. Fuel planning is done very conservatively as you can see. However, some fearful flyers remember the Avianca flight that crashed at New York's Kennedy Airport. That plane was put into a holding pattern, never declared an emergency, and ran out of fuel. If the pilot had declared a fuel emergency, the airspace around the airport would have been cleared and the flight would have been allowed to land immediately. No one knows why the pilot allowed the plane to run out of fuel and crash, but it was unnecessary. As noted in Chapter 5, Avianca is one of the world's least safe airlines. Perhaps the pilot did not know that he could declare an emergency. Perhaps he spoke English too poorly to declare an emergency. This could not have happened to a U.S. airplane or to any of the others that I have listed as the safest airlines in the world.

What happens if bad weather develops en route?

The captain is in charge of the flight and any changes that occur after it takes off. If bad weather is detected on radar, the pilot contacts air traffic control and requests an alternate route, which is provided. The pilot may also contact the dispatcher for advice on this matter.

*I don't like to fly to Europe or Asia because
we spend so much time over water. What
can I do?*

Flying to Europe of Asia you do spend a lot of time over water, but remember that no U.S. commercial carrier has ever landed in water in the jet age, which began in the late fifties. It may also be helpful for you to know that you are never very far from land, particularly when you fly to Europe. When you look at a map of the world, it is usually flat, and you might think planes fly straight across the Atlantic Ocean to London or other European destinations. Find a globe and try to find the shortest route to London. You will find that it parallels the coast of Canada, is near Greenland, and in fact never is far from land. Now for a little bit of trivia. If you fly to Hawaii, the halfway point between Los Angeles and Honolulu is the point at which you are farthest from land no matter where you fly in the world.

*Why are planes with two engines allowed
to fly to places like Hawaii and Europe?
Wouldn't it be safer to fly planes with four
engines like the B-747?*

Some fearful flyers only book overseas flights on four-engine aircraft, but this is getting to be extremely difficult. At one time the airlines were permitted to use only four-engine planes to fly to Europe and Hawaii. However, because of advances in technology, jet engines became more reliable and three -engine planes such as the DC-10 were cleared for flight to Europe and Asia. Now, engines are so reliable that many pilots will never experience an engine failure in their careers, and two-engine planes have been approved for flights to Europe.

*Are there any differences in safety between
flying at night and flying during the day?*

Flying at night is just as safe as flying during the day. Some fearful flyers like to fly during the day so they can keep an eye on the ground. Others like to fly at night so they cannot tell how far up they are. You will realize that your fear of flying is behind you when you don't worry about when you fly, or what equipment you are on, and you do not watch the weather forecast. More about weather later.

Why do planes fly so high?

Many fearful flyers would feel better if the plane flew closer to the ground. The fact is that this would make the flight less safe for a number of reasons. First, there are fewer planes at higher altitudes, so the risk of midair collision is all but eliminated. Second, the higher a plane is flying, the farther it can glide in the one in trillion chance that all engines should fail. There is one other reason why jets fly at high altitudes: jet engines run more economically at higher altitudes than they do at low altitudes.

What do you mean when you say that every aspect of the flight is controlled?

Let's consider a typical flight. After all passengers are on board and in their seats, a flight attendant must inform the pilot that everyone is seated. It is illegal for the pilot to move the plane with anyone standing. Before the plane can be moved from the jet bridge, permission must be gained from ramp control. Once the plane is pushed back from the jet bridge, the pilot must obtain permission from ground control before he or she can begin to taxi. Once the end of the runway is reached, the pilot must get clearance from the tower control to take off. When the plane is in the air, the pilot must get permission from air traffic control to deviate from the prescribed flight plan unless there is an emergency.

During all phases of the flight, including the taxi out in major airports, the plane is on radar. Its speed, course, and altitude are recorded every step of the way. In addition, instruments on board the plane monitor every aspect of the flight and record them. The cockpit voice recorder records every word that is said in the cockpit. If pilots make errors, such as flying too fast or wandering off course, and they do not have a conference with a member of the highway patrol, they are automatically subject to violation. This is the equivalent of your being monitored automatically from the moment you get into your car in your garage until you arrive at work, day after day, after day.

I've heard that pilots are risk takers. How do I know that they are attending to the business of flying the plane?

First, pilots are among the most conservative group of professionals in U.S. society. As one pilot puts it, "We are conservative economically, politically, and most of all, when we have the lives of others in our hands."

But back to the question. After the crash of an Eastern Airlines airplane in a swamp outside of Miami, the NTSB investigation revealed that the crew had all become involved in trying to locate the source of a problem that had developed, and no one was really attending to flying the airplane. Another accident investigation revealed that the crew was discussing their stock portfolios. Subsequently, the FAA mandated what is called a *sterile cockpit period*, which begins with departure from the jet bridge and continues to 10,000 feet. It begins again at 10,000 feet on descent and ends when the plane is safely parked at the jet bridge. During this period the crew cannot be interrupted by the flight attendants, are prohibited from making announcements other than those that pertain to the safety of the flight, and must refrain from engaging in conversations other than those related to the flight.

In addition, the crew works as a team to solve any problems that develop in order to ensure that someone is responsible for flying the aircraft. Remember, everything said in the cockpit is recorded and, in the case of an incident, the recorder is used to determine what occurred in the cockpit. Also remember that pilots are professionals. They will obey the rules not only because their job and their own safety is involved, but because they take pride in doing a job well.

Weather

Some types of weather pose a threat to airplanes. Advances in technology and training have enabled the industry to minimize this threat. Some fearful flyers anxiously watch the weather channel and cancel their flights at the first sign of rain or other inclement weather. I don't, because I know that the dispatcher and the crew are watching the weather for me.

Many airports have trouble with fog limiting the visibility of pilots. Is it safe to land in low visibility?

The general rule here is that if the pilot is making the landing, it is safe. However, the rules governing low visibility landings are complex. First, the rules depend on the nature of the runway. Is it equipped with an electronic glide slope so that an instrument landing is possible? If yes, a low visibility landing is possible. Second, the pilots' length of service and training determine whether a low visibility landing is possible. New pilots are restricted to making landings when the ceiling (distance between the base of the clouds and the ground) is at least 300 feet.

The third factor governing low-visibility landings is the equipment on board the plane. Some planes are equipped to land in *0/0 conditions.* This means that they can land with zero ceiling and a forward visibility of 600 feet as measured by an instrument on the runway. Ultimately, 0/0 will mean just that; no ceiling and no forward visibility.

How is a 0/0 landing possible?

Electronics and computers make this possible. These landings are done by autopilots that interpret an electronic signal. The autopilot adjusts the speed of the airplane using autothrottles; adjusts the control surfaces on the wings as the plane lands; and applies the brakes on landing. The pilot's job is to monitor the operation, and yes, there is more than one autopilot.

What about ice on the planes? I know some accidents have been caused by failure to deice planes properly.

A 1982 Air Florida crash in Washington, D.C. and a 1987 Continental Airlines crash in Denver were linked in part to faulty deicing. A more recent USAir commuter crash at New York's La Guardia Airport, which was initially thought to have resulted from faulty deicing, was attributed more to pilot error than icing, after the National Transportation Safety Board investigation. However, new rules governing deicing should eliminate icing as a problem.

Three significant changes in deicing have occurred since 1993. One of these is that the warm water and glycol deicing fluid used to deice planes contains more glycol than it did prior to 1993, and so the likelihood that ice will remain after deicing is eliminated. Second, after deicing, planes are coated with a solution that will keep ice from forming for a longer period of time than was previously the case. Third, the amount of time between deicing and takeoff has been reduced. Airlines such as American Airlines also do visual inspections of the areas of the planes that are susceptible to icing prior to takeoff. The FAA and the airline industry can be criticized for not implementing these steps earlier, but the important point is that they have been implemented.

*What about ice on the runway? Isn't hazardous
to land when the runways are slick?*

Unsafe runways are closed until they can be cleared, by removing the snow or other means. Also, as snow and ice develop, crews inspect the runways regularly to determine whether they are safe. Finally, planes are equipped with antilock/antiskid braking systems that prevent them from locking up and causing the plane to skid. In 1982 a World Airlines plane skidded off the runway into the bay at Boston's Logan Airport, killing two people. As noted earlier, a USAir commuter accident that was thought to be the result of icing, either on the plane or the runway, was probably only remotely related to the icing problem.

*What about ice on the wings of the aircraft?
I read that an American Eagle ATR-72
crashed because ice formed on the wings.*

Icing during the flight can be a problem for some small planes, but not for the modern jetliner. Why? Because airplanes that fly using jet engines (as opposed to those that use jet engines to turn propellers) circulate heat from those engines through the wings and other areas that might collect ice. Smaller, propeller-driven planes do not have this system. However, most planes, with the exception of the ATR-72, have very effective deicing systems. The problem experienced by the ATR-72 commuter aircraft is being corrected at the time this is being written.

*What about thunderstorms? Aren't they
dangerous?*

Yes, thunderstorms are dangerous. The center of a thunderstorm contains high winds, hail, and heavy rain. The industry's approach to dealing with them is avoidance. At altitude, commercial aircraft must remain twenty miles from the core of a thunderstorm. The *core* is defined as the red area that you see on TV when your local channel reports on the storm and that pilots see on their weather radar.

Many people report flying through thunderstorms. They tell of seeing lightning, hearing thunder, and being in heavy rain. They are probably right. Remember, if there is no heavy turbulence, it is legal and safe to fly in the light green, dark green, and even the yellow areas of rainstorms that you see on your television. However, because pilots want to give you a comfortable ride, they will typically avoid the yellow areas because they often contain bumpy air.

What would happen if the pilot inadvertently flew into a thunderstorm?

This isn't going to happen, but I asked some pilots this question. Some of them, when they were in the military, actually looked for thunderstorms to fly into when they were being pursued by enemy pilots who wanted to kill them. Others flew into thunderstorms to see what they were like. Their reports of flying through thunderstorms always contain one phrase: highly turbulent. Airplanes are not going to come apart in the red area of a thunderstorm. They may get beaten up by large hail and the damage may amount to thousands of dollars, but the wings will not fall off and they will continue to fly. You would not be hurt if you had your seat belt on and the plane flew into a thunderstorm; but you would be shaken up.

If you really want to know how a plane functions in a thunderstorm, contact the U.S. Weather Bureau to obtain a copy of the videotapes made by planes known as *hurricane hunters*. Once a day the U.S. Weather Bureau sends a reconnaissance plane into each hurricane to take readings of wind velocity and other indicators of the intensity of the storm. These planes must fly through embedded thunderstorms and high winds. The crew looks as if they are in a blender, but the plane survives quite nicely. You also need to know that the hurricane hunters are not specially built for the purpose of flying into thunderstorms.

What happens if lightning strikes a plane?

The fact is that lightning will probably strike a plane somewhere in the world today and every day. The plane will survive with no ill effects because it is not connected to the ground. As a result the lightning simply "passes through" the plane and produces no ill effects to the plane and the passengers. The people on board the plane will be scared because the lightning strike is likely to be accompanied by a flash and a loud peal of thunder. If this happens to you, just tell your neighbor (and yourself), "It's okay, planes get struck by lightning every day. They aren't grounded."

I've heard that wind shear is associated with thunderstorms and that it can cause accidents. Is this true?

Technically, wind shear is a condition in which the wind direction and/or velocity changes rather dramatically in a short distance and in a short time span. Wind shear at higher altitudes is not dangerous. However, at lower elevations it presents a potential hazard to airplanes, and yes, it is often associated with thunderstorms. Actually, there is a special and very dangerous type of wind shear called a *microburst* that is most worrisome. The type of microburst most often described in the media begins with a strong head wind and is followed by a tail wind, torrents of rain, and a strong downdraft that literally slams the plane into the ground if the pilot does not take evasive action. Other types of microburst can be equally dangerous. A microburst caused the crash of Delta Airlines L-1011 in Dallas (1985) and more recently, the crash of a USAir DC-9 in Charlotte, North Carolina (1994).

Dealing with Wind Shear

The airlines and the FAA have instituted several measures to help pilots deal with wind shear. One of these is changes in the training pilots receive. Currently pilots are taught to recognize wind shear conditions in flight simulators and to avoid them by taking evasive action. Every six months captains take refresher training in making these maneuvers. In addition, two wind shear detection devices have been developed. One of these is a device that measures wind speed and velocity. This has been placed around runways, and when it detects the presence of wind shear conditions, air traffic controllers are warned. The second method of detecting wind shear is Doppler radar, which you may have seen on your local television weather show.

Unfortunately, the best of these devices, Doppler radar, has not been installed at many airports. It seems likely that the crash of the USAir plane in Charlotte would have been averted if the airport had been equipped with Doppler radar. However, the Charlotte crash might also have been avoided if the air traffic controllers and pilots had acted differently. Information about the seriousness of the wind shear in the area was not relayed properly to the pilots, and the pilots flying the plane made a serious error when they reacted to the wind shear. USAir has revamped its training procedures to help their pilots deal more effectively with wind shear in the future.

Should you worry about wind shear? I do not believe that you should, based on probability. In the last decade about 100 million airplanes have taken off and landed in this country and two of them have been lost to wind shear. Many pilots believe that the likelihood of a wind shear accident happening in the future is practically nil. USAir was criticized by the FAA because of the training they provided to their pilots, and they have improved in this area. Procedures for informing the pilots about the presence of wind shear have improved as well. The final step, the installation of Doppler radar at all airports and the development of new detection devices for onboard use, should eliminate wind shear as a safety hazard. The FAA has purchased these devices. Local problems are slowing their installation, but they should be in use in the near future.

> *I worry that pilots are pressured by*
> *their companies to fly in bad weather*
> *to maintain schedules. Is this true?*

Once the captain signs the flight plan, he or she accepts full responsibility for that flight. In operating the flight, the captain has the following concerns in order of priority: safety, passenger comfort, and schedule. Captains are required to make responsible decisions, but because of their training and professionalism, decisions regarding safety are rarely questioned unless they make a mistake that results in an accident. Most importantly, they are not hassled by their companies about on-time arrivals.

It may also help you to understand that most pilots get paid by the minute. If they push back and wait thirty minutes for a thunderstorm to pass before flying to their destination, they make more money than they do if there is no delay. One pilot told me that one of his colleagues would look over and say "Ca-Ching," as though he was placing money in a cash register, when they had a weather delay. Safety is the first rule for captains, and they are naturally conservative because they care about their passengers and themselves. However, waiting on the weather can also make economic sense to the captain and the crew.

Turbulence

Turbulence is not a safety issue with the possible exception of the turbulence caused by the wingtip vortices of heavy aircraft. If a light plane lands too soon after a heavy plane it can result in an accident. If you encounter turbulence, just relax. The pilot will get you out of it as soon as possible.

> *What causes turbulence?*

There are a variety of factors that cause turbulence, but before I give them to you, please understand that *turbulence* is air in motion. It will help you visualize it if you stick a hose into a large container of water, turn the hose on, and watch the water: the water moves, which is exactly what happens when two streams of air come together. Most people imagine that air blends together smoothly because they cannot see it. This is not the case. Now to the causes of turbulence.

In the United States the prevailing wind direction is from west to east. As the wind encounters mountains, trees, and even buildings, it is forced to rise. In doing so it displaces other air, causing the air to move. Thunderstorms have tremendous amounts of energy and generate changes in air currents, which in turn causes other air to move. When a cold front from the north encounters warm air, because the cold air is heavier, it displaces the warm air, causing it to rise. This produces rain and also puts air into motion. On a warm day the sun warms the earth, causes moisture to evaporate, and air to rise (convective heating). As this air rises, it causes other air to move. When an airplane passes through the air, small whirlwind-like vortices spiral off the wingtips, displacing other air and thus setting it into motion. Wind, the heating of the earth, thunderstorms, the movement of fronts, and airplanes cause turbulence. So does the jet stream, at least on the edges where the jet stream is moving faster than the air around it.

Does turbulence pose a threat to airplanes?

Turbulence is not a threat to airplanes. Most fearful flyers believe that, in turbulence, the wings may come off, or the pilot will be unable to control the plane and it will go spiraling into the ground. To those of you who believe this, I challenge you to identify one U.S. plane that has been knocked out of the sky by turbulence. There haven't been any.

I have read stories about people being injured by turbulence. What happened?

First of all, it is not always possible to predict turbulence. Typically, turbulence occurs over mountain ranges, near thunderstorms, and over very warm areas, such as Phoenix, Arizona in the summer time. However, there is a phenomenon known as clear air turbulence (CAT) which, while it is often associated with sharp turns in the jet stream, can occur in other situations. A plane can fly into CAT, and passengers who are not belted into their seats can hit the ceiling or have hot coffee spilled on them. That is why you are advised by the pilot to keep your seat belt fastened. That is also why experienced flyers hang on to a seat back as they walk about the cabin. You need not fear turbulence, but you should be prepared for it because it is always possible that you will encounter some during a flight.

The next time you read about passengers being injured in turbulence, look carefully to see if some of the injured were flight attendants. They are in greatest jeopardy when a plane hits turbulent air because they are not seated. Do not be alarmed if the pilot asks the flight attendants to take their seats. This is being done for their safety, not because some terrible catastrophe is about to befall the aircraft.

Is it possible to measure turbulence?

Pilots are provided with a turbulence index for each segment of the flight on every flight plan. The index used for these estimates ranges from one to six. You will never experience level six turbulence because it is illegal to dispatch a plane into it. However, I will provide you with your own turbulence meter so you can measure the turbulence you experience.

On your next flight, ask the flight attendant to bring you a glass of water. Place it on the tray in front of you. If there is nothing more than an occasional ripple, you are flying in zero level turbulence. If the ripples become more frequent, but the water does not spill, you are in level one or two turbulence. If the water begins to slosh out of the glass, you are probably in level four turbulence. In level four turbulence you will feel the plane move from side to side a bit and you may seem to move upward against your seat belt. I repeat, you are in no danger, but I do not guarantee that you will be comfortable.

How do pilots feel about turbulence?

Typically, pilots don't like turbulence, not because it is dangerous, but because they are professionals who want to give you a comfortable ride. They will do their best to find an altitude that is relatively smooth, and you may feel the plane climb or descend as they change altitudes to find smoother air. The one exception to this rule came from one pilot who flew planes to Tokyo at the end of his career. He confessed that he actually enjoyed a little "light chop" after sitting for a while because it restored circulation to his back side.

I have read about planes that were upended because they landed too close to others. Why did this occur?

Wingtip vortices, when they come off the tips of the wings of large planes, can be forceful enough to upend small planes. This is a problem on landing. However, wingtip vortices move or dissipate fairly quickly, so planes are spaced from two to five minutes apart to eliminate this threat. If you are landing behind a small plane, such as a Fokker 100, a Boeing 737 or 727, or McDonnell Douglas-built DC-9-80, you will be flying two to three miles behind it. If you are flying behind a Boeing 747, 757, or 767, a DC-10 or other "heavy" airplane, the spacing will be greater, probably at least five miles.

What is an air pocket?

An air pocket is a figment of a journalist's active mind. The term air pocket was apparently coined during World War I by a journalist trying to describe turbulence. Many fearful flyers believe that there are "holes in the sky," which if flown into, will result in the plane falling hundreds, if not thousands, of feet. There are no air pockets.

If there are no air pockets, why do planes fall hundreds of feet?

It is literally impossible for a plane to fall hundreds of feet, even though it may seem to you and to others that you are falling long distances. The only reliable indicator of how far a plane moves in turbulence is the altimeter located in the cockpit. I have talked with pilots with many years of flying experience about planes falling. Most of them have never seen the altimeter move more than 20 feet in the heaviest turbulence. One reported a movement of 50 feet. That is really not very far when a plane is flying at 25,000 feet.

It is also important to note that planes do not fall in turbulence in the sense that an elevator might fall—that is, they do not go straight down. A plane is moving forward at a speed of 450 to 550 miles per hour when flying at altitude. What happens to a plane in turbulence is not unlike what happens to you when you pass over a speed bump in your car. The car keeps going forward. One difference between the operation of your car and the operation of an airplane is that a speed bump or a pothole can cause the car to leave the road. Planes have no such problems.

Do pilots have trouble keeping planes under control in turbulence?

The image that most people have of the cockpit has been derived from movies such as *Airplane*, which depicts the pilot struggling with the yoke to maintain control of the plane in turbulence. In many instances the plane is on autopilot when flying through turbulence because the autopilot can sense the changes that are occurring in the air currents and make changes to compensate for them. However, pilots are perfectly capable of flying the airplane in all situations, including turbulence, and keeping it under control.

Terrorism and Bombs

Because of events such as the Oklahoma City bombing flyers' concerns about bombing and terrorism are understandably at an all time high. The information in this section will help you understand what is being done to protect you from terrorist attacks.

Who is involved in airport and airplane security?

The first line of defense against people who would damage airplanes and/or commit acts of terrorism is our local and state police and the Federal Bureau of Investigation. They keep suspected terrorists under surveillance as a preventive measure and follow up on warnings about terrorist acts. Some routes flown by U.S. carriers regularly have antiterrorist officers aboard in plain clothes. For obvious reasons these routes are not identified.

In addition, each airline has its own security forces. The most visible security force is made up of the personnel that operate the metal detectors to the entrance to every concourse in an airport. The alertness of these people is checked by security personnel who try to slip knives, guns, and mace, all of which are illegal, through the detectors. Some airports also have personnel with dogs that are trained to detect various types of explosives. Every airport has security guards that police the boundaries of the airport to prevent people from trespassing and boarding planes or sabotaging them in some way.

I'm concerned about bombs. Is luggage x-rayed?

Luggage that is placed aboard international flights is x-rayed, but luggage that is placed aboard domestic flights probably isn't x-rayed. One airline official told me that they x-ray some domestic luggage, but declined to tell me what percent is actually x-rayed. Of course, carry-on luggage is x-rayed, so the task of x-raying luggage only involves checked baggage.

Do airlines have other strategies for preventing terrorists' attacks?

On international flights, boarding passes are matched to luggage slips to ensure that only the luggage of the people on board the plane is placed on the plane. This is supposed to be a policy for some domestic carriers as well, but it is not a well-enforced policy.

What is the status of bomb detectors?

One bomb detection device has recently been certified by the FAA. It is called the CTX 5000 and uses the same technology found in CT-Scan devices found in hospitals. The cost of these devices is $865,000 each, and according to *Newsweek* (April 24, 1994), it would take 32 of them to examine all the luggage that passes through New York's Kennedy Airport. However, I was told by a representative of the FAA that higher-speed, lower-cost devices are in the works. You can speed the installation of these devices as well as increased security measures by airline companies by contacting your representatives in Congress. It is interesting to note that the American flying public has said repeatedly that they are willing to pay for safety.

Are other security measures in place?

Airline security begins with the hiring process. Background checks are conducted for every person who will be placed in positions dealing with the flight. This includes people hired at local airports. Secure areas are established in and around airports. Only people who have security clearances and identification badges can enter these areas without an escort.

Miscellaneous Questions

Fearful flyers are afraid of many things. In fact, collectively they are afraid of every aspect of flying. The personnel in the airline industry have another fear: that the industry will become unsafe. If that happens, their companies will declare bankruptcy and they will lose their jobs.

*I have heard that the quality of the air I
breathe in an airplane is so poor that I
might get ill. Is this true?*

In the last five years there have been many rumors spread via the media about the quality of air in airplanes. Here are some facts about the air in an airplane:

- Fresh air is brought into the airplane through the engines and dispersed through the air conditioning system. Old air is let out of the plane through a valve in the rear of the plane. (On one approach to Boston's Logan Airport you can smell bread baking in a bakery below.)

- The air is changed in the plane every three to ten minutes, depending upon the type of airplane.

- The pilots breathe the same air as the passengers.

- The Center for Disease Control in Atlanta has determined that you are in no greater risk of contacting a communicable disease on board an aircraft than you are in other places you visit. To be sure, you can catch a cold from the person next to you on an airplane, but you can also catch a cold if you visit an elementary school classroom.

There are some problems with the air in planes. One of these is that the air has very little humidity in it and this makes some people uncomfortable on long flights. Drink lots of water, lighten up on the alcohol, and take your contacts out if you wear them because they will dry out and make you uncomfortable. All these steps will help you adjust to the low humidity. It is also the case that the carbon dioxide level in planes exceeds that found in fresh air. The result of breathing this air for long periods of time can be headaches and fatigue, particularly on long flights.

*How can we still breathe when we are flying
at 35,000 feet?*

It is true that you could not get enough air into your lungs to survive at 35,000 feet unless some steps were taken to help you. In order to make sure that you can breathe, the cabin is pressurized by restricting the outward airflow. This allows you to breathe normally. Actually, sitting in an airplane at 35,000 feet is about the same as visiting Denver. The "altitude" of the cabin is about 6,500 feet.

What if the pressurization system fails?

Failure of the pressurization equipment is rare, but it does happen. In this event an oxygen mask drops out of an overhead compartment or the seat back in front of you. This should be placed over your nose and mouth and you should breathe normally. Immediately after depressurization, the pilot will take the plane down to an altitude that will allow you to breathe normally, This will typically be 10,000 feet or less. I once flew from Atlanta, Georgia to Raleigh-Durham, North Carolina on a plane that had broken pressurization equipment. We flew at an altitude of 7,000 feet and were perfectly comfortable.

I have heard that airplanes sometimes fly into flocks of birds. If this is true, what is the result?

It is true that planes fly into birds of all types from time to time. The result is typically a dead bird. Many years ago birds posed a safety hazard to airplanes, but this is not true anymore. Why? Because engines have been improved to the point that they can ingest birds and continue to function. In fact, engines are tested by firing dead chickens into them. It is still possible for a large bird or a flock of birds to damage an engine, and one engine may have to be shut down. However, a Southwest Airlines B-737 encountered an entire flock of Canadian geese and still landed safely. The FAA requires that when planes are built, they must be able to sustain a strike with an eight-pound bird and still remain airworthy. Manufacturers exceed this requirement.

Where is the safest place to sit on an airplane?

Typically when fearful flyers ask this question they mean, where is the safest place to be in a crash? First, all places on an airplane are safe, but the FAA told me that no one place is safer than another in a crash. Sixty percent of people involved in crashes survive no matter where they are sitting.

Are some airports safer than others?

There are consistent rumors that some airports are unsafe. This is simply untrue. The FAA would close an unsafe airport. Do some airports require a pilot to exercise more skills than others? Pilots think that New

York's La Guardia Airport and Washington, D.C.'s National Airport fit into this category. Does this make them more dangerous? One pilot who was asked this question responded with, "I've landed airplanes on aircraft carriers, now that requires some skill." The point: some airports require more skill during landing and takeoff, but they do not come close to exceeding the pilots' skills who take off and land there every day. The stories written about dangerous airports were written by uninformed journalists who often use faulty data for their articles.

What if there is an emergency when the plane is in the air?

There are two types of emergencies that might occur: one involving a passenger and one involving the plane. As you know, the pilot will land the plane at the nearest airport if a passenger becomes ill. The same is true if a mechanical problem develops. The pilot may or may not inform you of the emergency, depending on the workload in the cockpit. I'm sure you would rather have the crew attending to business in the cockpit than talking to you.

How likely is it that I will be in an emergency evacuation?

Richard Gross, a former pilot, compiled some statistics on the incidence and outcomes of emergency landings for the 1987 to 1993 period, which were included in an article by Betsy Wade in the *New York Times*. He identified 169 emergency evacuations during that time, or fewer than 30 per year. Since there were approximately 10.5 million flights per year, that means that your chances of being in an emergency evacuation are about 1 in 350,000 each time you fly. Over 600 people out of nearly 16,000 evacuees sustained some type of injury, although only about 100 received injuries more serious than a bruise or an abrasion.

How can I avoid an injury if I am in an emergency evacuation?

Earlier I recommended that you pay very careful attention to the flight attendants in these situations because they are well trained to handle them. Some other recommendations include

- Take off high heels and panty hose. The high heels may catch on the slide or injure others. The panty hose will melt on the slide and give you a bad burn. Also remove rubber-soled shoes. They have a tendency to catch on the slides and cause people to tumble. Keep your shoes so that you can put them on quickly once you have evacuated.

- Wear clothing to cover all bare areas, especially below the waist. Never board a plane wearing shorts or a miniskirt. Do not put your hands down on the slide as you evacuate. Instead, fold them across your chest or hold them above your head. This will prevent painful abrasions from rubbing your hands against the slide.

- Once you are out of the plane, move quickly away from it. Many injuries occur because evacuating passengers run into people in the evacuation area.

- Wear cotton clothing. It will not melt and is less likely to tear on the slides.

- Forget about your belongings. Worry only about getting yourself out of the plane.

- Put infants in a car seat. It costs more money, but if the plane stops suddenly it is unlikely that you will be able to hold on to your child.

- If there is smoke in the plane (which is very, very rare) don't drop to the floor as you have been taught to do in household fires. Instead, bend over and lower your head to the point that it is about as high as your waist. This will allow you to be mobile and avoid the most noxious smoke.

What is the meaning of the announcement to turn off nonapproved electronic devices just before takeoff and during descent?

Some electronic devices, such as CD players, cellular phones, and personal computers, interfere with the navigational devices used by pilots. This interference, while potentially dangerous, has never caused an accident, but it has caused missed approaches and go-arounds. This interference is only a problem at low altitudes when very precise navigation is required, and thus these devices can be used safely at altitudes above 10,000 feet.

Summary

After reading Chapters 5 and 6, you know more about airplanes, crew members, and the technical aspects of flying than most members of the flying public. Perhaps the most important fact to hang on to is that the U.S aviation industry is the best in the world, and that every aspect of the flight is planned and carried out with safety in mind. Is it a perfect industry? No. But it is safer today than it was yesterday and it will be safer tomorrow than it is today. I believe that the biggest improvement in the safety in the long term will be in the commuter airlines, partially because they have more room for improvement.

You can help make sure that the airline industry becomes safer and safer. If your airport does not have Doppler radar installed, write to your representatives in the U.S. House and Senate. If you feel corners are being cut in some aspect of the industry, complain to the FAA. Most importantly, "vote" for safety by spending your money on those airlines that have the best safety records, and let them know that you are flying them because of their safety record. If you fly on airlines that have low safety records to save a few dollars, you are sending the wrong message.

Continue to add to the knowledge you have gained here as you recover from your fear of flying. However, beware of your sources of information. Make sure that you ask a pilot who flies for a major airline, the FAA, or the National Transportation Safety Board. Other sources of information may be faulty.

7

Coping with Anticipatory Anxiety

You get a call from your boss and she tells you that you have been selected to represent the company at a crucial meeting in Albuquerque next month. Your spouse comes home with a "wonderful" surprise: you're going to Paris to celebrate your anniversary. For most people, representing their company or traveling to Paris generates excitement. If you are afraid to fly and suffer from anticipatory anxiety, these announcements generate only one response: dread.

What Is Anticipatory Anxiety and Who Suffers From It?

As noted earlier, one very simple definition of anticipatory anxiety is that it is the fear of fear. You are not flying today, but you begin to think about the day you will fly, and it scares you and you begin to worry. Anticipatory anxiety begins with automatic, fearful thoughts such as, I'll die if I fly. In brief, you begin to worry. This produces an emotional state that varies tremendously from individual to individual. For some, thinking about the flight ahead brings only mild anxiety characterized by some muscle tension, an occasional headache, inability to concentrate for short periods of time, and perhaps a little sleep loss. For others, anticipatory anxiety may bring about some or all of the following symptoms: migraine headaches, severe intestinal distress, lower back pain, extreme insomnia, irritability, and nightmares of horrible events during what is usually restless sleep.

Just as there is considerable variation in the symptoms experienced by people who have anticipatory anxiety about flying, there are differences in when the anticipatory anxiety begins. A French lawyer could not concentrate well enough to practice law if he had a flight scheduled within a year, and he invariably canceled all his flights. However, this is an extreme case. For most people, anxiety about flying does not set in until a week or so before the flight. It usually begins with mild anxiety and then builds to intense anxiety the night before the flight. This may result, in addition to the symptoms just listed, in emotional outbursts. The night before we were scheduled to fly, my wife would routinely accuse me of trying to kill her by making her fly. Of course, I was getting on the same plane.

How Do You Rid Yourself of Anticipatory Anxiety?

Unfortunately, anxiety about flying does not subside once you reach your initial destination. You may have summoned the courage to fly to an exotic spot that you always wanted to visit, only to spend your vacation worrying about the return flight or looking for alternate ways to get home. While not everyone experiences anticipatory anxiety, if you do, you will understand why I call it the most painful part of the fear of flying. It doesn't just make you uncomfortable during the flight, which is often of short duration. Anticipatory anxiety makes you miserable for days, and sometimes weeks.

One of the oddities about anticipatory anxiety is that it does not go away simply because you fly without fear. Many fearful flyers seek treatment primarily because of their anticipatory anxiety. They often report, "Once they close the door, I'm okay." Other fearful flyers report that after treatment they can fly in comfort, but they still experience anticipatory anxiety. You should assume that your anticipatory anxiety has a life of its own and must be treated if you are to recover.

If you do not deal with your anticipatory anxiety, and it is intense, the probability is that sooner or later you will eventually avoid flying altogether because of the discomfort. If you experience mild anticipatory anxiety, you may be able to tolerate it and keep on flying, but why accept the discomfort? You can defeat the anxiety using one of the strategies presented in this chapter. A discussion of which of the two strategies may be best for you follows the presentation. However, before outlining the strategies for defeating anticipatory anxiety, I want to discuss what not to do.

To Suppress or Not to Suppress

Suppression is the process of either diverting your thoughts about flying, through tactics such as listening to music or working crossword puzzles, or systematically "not owning" your fearful thoughts. When you are not thinking about flying, you have no anxiety and are more comfortable. Because your comfort level goes up when you suppress, you may begin to engage actively in various suppression approaches. The problem: suppression is not curative and often doesn't work except for very short periods of time.

I have been told by dozens of people, "I don't think I have anticipatory anxiety. I don't worry." However, when I question these people, some of them admit that they do not sleep as well before a flight, they experience stomach distress, and they may get stress headaches. Some fearful fliers even go as far as ignoring the physical symptoms associated with anxiety, because those symptoms cue scary thoughts.

Suppression is a losing battle. Try this. Tell yourself not to think about solving an important problem that needs attention in the very near future. If you are like most people, it will be virtually impossible to put it out of your mind. The harder you try to suppress the thought, in fact, the more often it occurs. If you are able to suppress thoughts about important problems, you have developed a skill that is counterproductive to overcoming irrational fear. You will need to work hard not to suppress your scary thoughts about flying.

The techniques outlined in the subsequent sections of this chapter are based on the idea that you need to invite your fear into your thoughts and then deal with it. If you are one of those people who does not know what it is about flying that scares you, begin immediately to identify those things about air travel that scare you. Accurate identification of your scary thoughts is essential in the process of eliminating your anticipatory anxiety, as well as dealing with your fear on the plane.

Strategy One: Worry Time

Worry time is a paradoxical strategy that may not make sense to you because it involves prescribing the symptom (worry). If you do not fully understand the rationale behind worry time, don't be concerned. The best minds in the mental health field are not sure why it works. The important thing for you to remember is that it does work!

Identify Your Fears

How do you use worry time? Begin by making a complete list of the things that scare you about flying. If you are afraid of the airplane and do not have any other problems, your list might contain these items:

- The mechanics do not repair the planes properly.
- Many airlines are flying old airplanes that are unsafe.
- The planes will fall apart in turbulence.
- The landing gear may not come down and we will crash.
- If I die my children will have no one to care for them.

If you are afraid of heights, you might have the following list:

- Turbulence will cause the plane to fall.
- The plane is so flimsy, I'll fall through the floor.
- The feeling I get when the pilot announces that we are at 35,000 feet is unbearable.
- I'll be up in the air for two hours with nothing supporting me, and we will fall.

If you are claustrophobic, you might have the following list:

- It will be hot and uncomfortable in the jet bridge and I won't have enough air.
- They will run out of air during the flight and I will suffocate.
- I can breathe for one hour, which is the scheduled time, but there will probably be a delay and I'll suffocate.

If you have panic attacks, you may have a list such as:

- As soon as they close that door I'm trapped.
- I'll have a panic attack, and I'll go crazy because there is no place to go.

- I'll have a panic attack and break out the glass in the windows.

- I'll have a panic attack and make a complete fool of myself and be totally embarrassed.

Of course, your list will be made up of other fears and may contain some of the fears from two or three of the sample lists. The important thing is that you develop as complete a list as possible at this time. You can add to it later, and I encourage you to do so. Use the space provided on the next page to identify the things that scare you about air travel.

Establish a Time to Worry

You now have a list of the things that frighten you most about air travel. The next step is to set aside two ten-minute periods each day, one in the morning and one in the early evening, to worry. I suggest that you use the time when you are preparing to go to work as your first worry time and then a time just after dinner for the second worry session.

Do not choose a time just before sleeping for a worry session. Why? Because if you worry properly, it will upset you. You will get in touch with your fear, and the anxiety will disturb your sleep. You need time to relax before sleeping, and thus it is best to schedule worry time in the early evening. If you are not on a typical nine-to-five schedule (for example, if you work midnight to eight in the morning), select a time just after you sleep and a few hours before you return to bed (for example, four o'clock and eleven o'clock).

Rules for Worrying

I know from experience that some of you are beginning to ask yourselves, "Is he serious?" Absolutely. Worry time, like all effective techniques, has procedures and rules that must be followed if it is to be effective. Here are the rules for worry sessions:

1. Worry in a place where you will not be overheard.

2. Worry aloud.

3. Worry in front of a mirror if possible.

4. Do not contradict yourself even if you believe you have said something infinitely foolish. Avoid rational thinking and concentrate on getting your irrational beliefs out.

5. Worry for the entire ten minutes, even if you run out of anything to worry about in a minute or so.

6. Don't call yourself stupid or silly before, during, or after the worry session.

7. Try to get in touch with the hook that drives your fear (dying, looking foolish, for example) and thus the emotion associated with your fear. Verbalize the hook during your worry sessions.

8. Restrict your worry sessions to fears about flying.

9. Worry twice a day until the anxiety begins to subside and then reduce the worry sessions to once a day. There is one exception to this rule:
   Do not worry the night before an early morning flight or on the day of a flight.

Why? Because it may increase your anticipatory anxiety about flying and increase the likelihood that you will avoid the flight.

   If you follow these rules, you will look at your watch, note the time, and begin to worry aloud.

My Fears About Air Travel

Turbulence

Sounds of unfamiliar noises during flight

Mechanical failure

Sense of having no control

Sample Worry Session: One Fear

If you have only one fear, the entire session will be devoted to that topic. For example, the common misperception that turbulence creates unsafe flying conditions and the plane will crash as a result might be addressed as follows:

> I know the book says that turbulence has never caused a plane to crash, but what does he know. The plane is unstable in turbulence, will get out of control and crash, and I will die. The worst part will be that last twenty seconds when I know I'm going to die and I can do nothing. I'll be totally out of control. And if the pilot can control it, one of the wings will drop off, and then she will not be able to control it. I remember on my last flight the wings were bouncing all around when we were in turbulence. The captain has no control over the bolts in those wings and they could certainly come loose. I saw that long-haired mechanic looking at our plane on my last flight. How do we know that he fastened those bolts properly? Why would they trust a person with long hair and a beard to work on planes? He is probably on drugs.

> Repeat if elapsed time is less than ten minutes.

Sample Worry Session: Many Fears

Of course, if you have several fears, your worry session will be more complex, but I have rarely found that the session takes more than ten minutes. In fact, most people are surprised that they can verbalize their fears, in a few minutes. If you have several fears your worry sessions might be like this:

> I hate airplanes. They are so small and cramped and people are packed into them like sheep. It gets so warm in them, and there is not enough air for all those people to breathe. I get that tight feeling in my chest every time I get on a plane. And they are constructed so poorly. In turbulence the overhead luggage compartments shake and even come open. When you walk down the aisle, you can feel the floor flex, they are built so poorly. I feel like I'm going to fall through the floor every time I get up, so I don't go to the lavatory and I get so uncomfortable. Once I thought I was going to soil myself, and now I think about that and think how embarrassing that would be.

I'll never put myself in that situation again. Mostly though, it's the terror I feel because I know that any second I will die. I sit very quietly, listening to every sound and watching the flight attendants. They are taught to smile even in the worst conditions, but they would show fear if something is really wrong with the airplane.

Repeat if elapsed time is less than ten minutes.

What to Do Between Worry Sessions

Purchase a small notebook to carry with you between worry sessions. I want you to write down any worrisome thoughts you have about flying. I'm not kidding—I do not want you to forget your worrisome thoughts. This is particularly true if a *new* worrisome thought pops up between worry sessions. By writing down your scary thoughts, you may begin to get a better idea about what your primary fears about flying are.

After you have written the scary thought down, simply say to yourself, "I'll worry about that in my next worry session," and dismiss it. This works very much like the list-making that people are taught in time management courses. If you have something on a list, and a time to deal with it, it gets to be less of a problem.

How Will You Know It's Working?

Before you begin worry time, answer the following questions:

1. How many days before a scheduled flight do I begin to worry?

2. What are the symptoms associated with my anticipatory anxiety? What is the intensity of anxiety as measured by my SUDS? Recall the physical symptoms such as tense muscles, shallow breathing, racing heart, heart palpitations, dizziness, headaches, diarrhea, and so on, which you measured in Chapter 4. If sleeplessness is a problem, when does it begin?

Answers to these questions can provide a baseline for judging your progress.

How long it will take to see results depends on two variables: the intensity of your anxiety and how compulsive you are about completing your worry sessions. It could take from a few weeks to several months. You should see some progress within four to six weeks if you follow the rules for worry sessions listed earlier.

You will know it's working, and you will stop when your anticipatory anxiety is either gone or when it is tolerable. The French lawyer I mentioned earlier stopped worry time after his anticipatory anxiety was reduced to the point that it occurred in a very mild form the night before a flight. Another fearful flyer stopped when she got tired of hearing herself worry about things that were totally irrational. You should stop when you reach your own comfort level.

Returning to Worry Time

Most people who overcome their anticipatory anxiety will not have relapses. However, some do, usually because they read or watch a detailed account of a plane accident or encounter something during a flight that scares them. If this happens to you, begin worry time immediately.

Strategy Two: Disputing Irrational Beliefs

Several mental heath professionals, including Aaron Beck and Albert Ellis, have highlighted the fact that our fearful, anxiety-producing thoughts are the result of irrational beliefs. Zig Ziglar, a motivational speaker, may have a better term for these beliefs. He calls them "stinkin' thinkin'." Worry time is one approach to dealing with your irrational thoughts. Another approach is to dispute them systematically as they occur. When you use this approach you literally talk back to your fear.

Almost all fearful flyers play mind games with their fear. For example, many fearful people understand that F-E-A-R is an acronym for False Evidence Appearing to be Real when it comes to airplanes. But in their games, the fear usually wins and the false evidence is believed. However, when you begin to use disputing statements, you begin to teach yourself new responses to your fearful thoughts.

Initial Steps

The first step in disputing irrational beliefs is much like beginning worry time: make a list of your irrational beliefs. The second step involves using information you trust to write rejoinders to the fearful thoughts. The key word in the foregoing sentence is *trust*. As has been mentioned many times, most fearful flyers have a lot of inaccurate information about flying and what will happen to them on a plane. If you do not trust the information you have, it will be of no value to you when you dispute the accuracy of your fearful thoughts.

Adding Emotion

At least two emotions are antithetical to fear and can be included in disputing statements. Humor will make you happy and break the power of your fear. Anger directed at your fear (remember: never at yourself) focuses your attention, energizes you, and allows you to confront your fear with more confidence.

Each person has a different sense of humor. To use humor, you must understand your own sense of humor and how to activate it. One way might be to exaggerate the danger. You may tell yourself that your plane is so dangerous it is likely to fall out of the sky while it is taxiing. Then conjure up a mental image of your plane "falling" through the runway as it taxis. Sometimes just stringing several absurd thoughts together will become humorous:

> With my luck, the plane is bound to crash. When I throw a penny into the air it lands on its side. I can't even get a head or a tail. My pilot is probably from the remnants of the Japanese kamikaze squads. He's so inept he crashed into a battleship and lived. When I get on board, the flight attendants will be wearing parachutes, this flight is so dangerous.

You may be able to think of other humorous thoughts that will break the tension produced by your fear. After you have broken the tension with humor, dispute your thoughts with accurate information.

Most people will probably find it easier to activate anger. As mentioned in Chapter 4, anger is often associated with profanity, and thus using swear words in your disputing statements may be all you need to become angry at your fear. It may help to consider how your fear has affected you to become angry. Perhaps it has cost you a job or a promotion, damaged an important relationship, or kept you from seeing the beauty of the world. If another person did that to you, you'd be *angry*! Do not direct this anger at yourself and call yourself names. Aim it at the alien in your mind—your fear.

Some Sample Lists of Fears and Disputing Statements

The following lists represent the irrational fears of many people who are afraid to fly. The sample disputing statements illustrate how accurate information and antithetical emotions can be used to counter those fears. If you use humor in your statements make sure that it does not detract from the value of the information included in the statement. (Try to identify my feeble attempts at injecting humor into the disputing statements.)

Person With Panic Attacks

Irrational belief:	I'll have a panic attack and do something crazy if I fly.
Disputing statement:	I may have a panic attack, but I can control my (expletive of your choosing) response, and I won't go crazy.
Irrational belief:	I'll have a panic attack and have a heart attack.
Disputing statement:	I may have a panic attack, but my heart is healthy. Besides, if I'm going to have a heart attack, a plane is the best place to be. The captain's responsibility is to get the best possible care as quickly as possible for sick passengers.
Irrational belief:	I'll have a panic attack and be catatonic for the rest of my life.
Disputing statement:	I won't become catatonic, but if I did, there would be no more slimnastics and wouldn't that be a hoot.
Irrational belief:	I'll take the train instead of the plane. At least if I have a panic attack I can pull the emergency cord and get off.
Disputing statement:	That's smart! You'll probably be in the middle of a Georgia swamp when you have the attack. You love snakes and alligators.

Person With Claustrophobia

Irrational belief:	If I fly, I'll run out of air and suffocate.
Disputing statement:	Not likely! The air is changed in the plane at least once every ten minutes.

Irrational belief:	When they close the door, I'll panic and hyperventilate.
Disputing statement:	No I won't. I know exactly how to control my breathing using the RED technique.
Irrational belief:	It's so hot and stuffy in that jet bridge I'll probably panic when I'm boarding the plane.
Disputing statement:	I'll be smart. I'll check in and then board the plane at the last minute.
Irrational belief:	If we have a delay, I'll panic.
Disputing statement:	Hell no, I won't panic. I can control my breathing.
Irrational belief:	The air is so stale in the plane it makes me sick.
Disputing statement:	No! The plane has plenty of fresh air. We'll probably smell the stockyards when we land in Chicago.

Person Who Is Acrophobic

Irrational belief:	If we hit turbulence, the plane will fall.
Disputing statement:	That's nonsense! No plane has ever been knocked out of the sky by turbulence.

or

Disputing statement:	Oh, sure. Planes fall out of the sky so often you have to wear a hard hat to keep plane parts from hitting you in the head.
Irrational belief:	After takeoff, when the captain lowers the nose, the sinking feeling I get scares me and I may panic.
Disputing statement:	Stop! That sensation is perfectly normal, and the plane isn't falling; it's climbing and accelerating.
Irrational belief:	The announcement that we have reached our cruising altitude of 35,000 feet scares me.

| Disputing statement: | Higher is safer. We are riding on solid columns of air and the plane *cannot* fall. |

Person Who Is Aviophobic

Irrational belief:	Most airlines are cutting corners because they are losing money.
Disputing statement:	Stop! Airlines lose money when they have accidents.
Irrational belief:	We'll fly into a thunderstorm and die.
Disputing statement:	Thunderstorms are dangerous, but the captain of the plane wants to get home just as much as I do.
Irrational belief:	If we get into clouds we'll have a midair collision.
Disputing statement:	Don't be silly! The air traffic controllers and traffic and collision avoidance system on board this plane will prevent midair collisions.
Irrational belief:	Flying is unsafe, and I will die if I get on a plane.
Disputing statement:	Jets are twenty times safer than automobiles, and commuters are just as safe as automobiles.
Irrational belief:	I'll cancel my reservation and drive. I'm in control then.
Disputing statement:	Stop it, you control freak. You are not in control of all those other drivers when you are in a car.

Now It's Your Turn

Enough examples. It's time for you to write down your irrational fears and disputing statements in the space provided on the next page, if you intend to use this strategy to deal with your anticipatory anxiety. As you write statements to dispute your fears, you may have to return to earlier chapters for the information you need. In the column marked with T (for trust), rate the extent to which you trust the information you use in the disputing statement. Use a 1–10 scale with a 1 meaning you do not trust the information at all and a 10 meaning that you almost completely trust the information that you have used. If this number is below 5, you should get additional information or information from other sources to increase your trust. See the reading list at the end of the book for sources of additional information about airplanes, panic attacks, claustrophobia, and acrophobia.

Disputing My Irrational Fears

T

Fear: _____

Disputing statement: _____

_____   ____

Fear: _____

Disputing statement: _____

_____   ____

Fear: _____

Disputing statement: _____

_____   ____

Using Disputing Statements

After you have written statements that dispute your irrational fears, it is time to begin using them to overcome your anticipatory anxiety. These thoughts may occur at various times, so be ready. One fearful flyer wrecked his car when he became so distracted by his thoughts that he forgot he was on a busy street. The procedure for using the thoughts is as follows:

1. Memorize the responses. If you think you will forget them, write them on adhesive note pads and put them in places such as the bathroom, the dash of your car, and around your work area.

2. Whenever a thought occurs, dispute it immediately.

3. Get angry!

Which Strategy To Use?

I suggest you choose either worry time or disputing your irrational thoughts depending entirely on which one seems most attractive to you. Some fearful flyers use a combination of the two—they use worry time twice a day and then dispute their thoughts between worry time. My concern about this approach is that you may overload yourself and stop using both strategies. Select one technique and use it!

For those times when one of these strategies isn't enough, I suggest two techniques already discussed:

- Use the RED technique (see Chapter 4) and control your breathing for five to seven minutes when your anxiety gets unbearable. This will be particularly important if your anticipatory anxiety keeps you awake. Sleeplessness can add to your anxiety because you worry about not getting enough sleep.

- Once you have slowed your breathing, scan your body and find tense muscles. Relax them by the identify, tense, relax method.

- Consider medication if your anxiety becomes intense. The exact type of medication should be determined by your doctor, but valium, xanex, klonopin, and ativan are some of the drugs often prescribed for this problem.

Remember that these drugs are addictive. If you have had problems with addictions, such as alcoholism, you may want to work especially hard on using the strategies described here before using drugs. Also, because they are addictive, if you take drugs regularly for anticipatory anxiety, you will need to withdraw from them slowly, probably over a period of weeks.

Summary

Anticipatory anxiety means that you worry before you need to—sometimes before the flight. The intensity and duration of anticipatory anxiety varies, as does the length of time needed to overcome the problem. Two strategies, worry time and disputing your fear, may be used to deal with the problem. It will generally take from a few weeks to a few months to lower the anxiety to a tolerable level if your anxiety has to do solely with flying. Controlling your breathing, muscle relaxation, and medication may also be useful in helping you deal with your anticipatory anxiety.

8

Coping on the Plane

The ultimate test in your fight to conquer the fear of flying is coping with the fear when you actually fly. This chapter is a dress rehearsal for your first successful flight. As you read this chapter, try to imagine yourself doing each of the described activities—from preflight planning to taxiing into the airport—and doing them with confidence. In Chapter 9 you will prepare a specific flight plan that addresses your fears. Then it will be time to tackle the monster in the air.

Preflight Planning

You now know that the pilot and dispatcher plan each flight carefully. You should also plan your flights, particularly if you have medical problems such as hypoglycemia (low blood sugar) or motion sickness. The food available on airplanes may not be suitable if you are hypoglycemic, and thus you need to pack your own. Motion sickness occurs because the inner ear sends faulty information to the brain. If you have motion sickness, you may already use over-the-counter products, such as dramamine and bonine. However, I recommend that you contact your doctor several days before your flight and get a prescription for much more effective remedies, such as antivert or valium.

Nasal congestion also needs to be taken into consideration as you plan your flight. You can fly if you are mildly congested if you use decongestant pills or nasal sprays. Use the latter if you have high blood pressure (many decongestants raise your blood pressure), or ask your pharmacist for a decongestant other than pseudoephedrine. It raises your blood pressure, elevates your heart rate, and may increase nervousness. Do not fly if you are severely congested because you may damage your inner ear. If you have any doubts about the extent of your congestion, contact your doctor.

Another aspect of preflight planning is packing. Consider compiling a list of clothing and personal items you wish to take on your trip. Trying to remember what you need just before the flight may be difficult. Remember, the brain doesn't function in the same way when you are fearful or anxious. Also, if you plan to take a taxi or limousine, call a day ahead to schedule the service and verify that the car will come on the day of the flight. The last thing you want is to miss your flight because of transportation problems, although you may have different thoughts at this time.

Getting to the Airport and Checking In

Before you leave home, contact the airline to verify that your flight is on time. It will only add to your anxiety if you arrive at the airport and find that your flight has been delayed. If it is on time, give yourself plenty of time to get to the airport if you are driving. Many people who are afraid to fly postpone their trip to the airport as long as possible. This is a mistake because unexpected traffic problems, difficulty finding a parking place, and long lines at baggage check-ins can raise their anxiety level. A good rule of thumb is to arrive at the terminal at least thirty minutes before departure for domestic flights and at least one hour ahead for international flights.

Make certain that you check in with the gate agent fifteen minutes before departure unless you already have your boarding pass. If you have a boarding pass, give your ticket to the person collecting tickets (usually a flight attendant) at least ten minutes prior to the flight. The gate agent can give your seat to someone else if you have not presented your ticket by that time, and regardless of how inviting it may seem now, you do not want to miss this flight.

As you board your flight, put your watch away and begin to attend only to your body and the flight. Many fearful flyers increase their fear by continuously looking at their watches, hoping that time is racing by.

Of course, you know what happens. The watch seems not to move at all and the flight lasts for an "eternity." Keep the watch where you can find it easily. You may need it later in the flight.

Boarding the Plane

With a few exceptions, such as Southwest Airlines, commercial air carriers board their planes by row numbers starting from the rear. Your seat and row number will be listed on your ticket. If you have checked in, you do not have to board the plane when your row number is called, and for some fearful flyers, it is best to board as late as possible.

For example, if you are claustrophobic or have panic attacks, you should board the plane as late as possible for two reasons. First, if you board with the other passengers, you are likely to find yourself packed into the jet bridge with a great many other people. This activates the fear of being trapped. The jet bridge can be extremely warm in the summertime—a condition that also activates fear of being trapped in many claustrophobics. Second, if you delay boarding the plane until the final boarding period, you can keep moving around, which may help lower your anxiety level.

Using Your Coping Techniques

When you do board the plane, go to your seat and make yourself as comfortable as possible. Make sure that you have your rubber band around your hand and directions for the RED technique where they are easily accessible. Leave nothing to your memory. You cannot remember facts when you are frightened. Once you are seated and your seat belt is securely fastened, check your SUDS score and begin to control your breathing using the RED technique. After five minutes, check your SUDS score again to see if you are making any progress.

Continue to control your breathing until you are well into the flight. If you cannot control your breathing, relax the muscles involved in the breathing process by using the identify, tense, relax method. If your heart is racing, you may also wish to use the Valsalva maneuver in conjunction with your breathing. (These relaxation techniques are all described in detail in Chapter 4.) You will construct a flight plan for yourself in the next chapter. However, controlling your breathing will be a part of all flight plans.

If you begin to have those scary, intrusive thoughts, use your rubber band with a vengeance. If it is properly placed over the palm of your hand, you cannot injure yourself. Use this weapon as often as necessary and accompany it with orders to yourself (injunctions) to *stop* thinking those scary thoughts. Remind yourself that you are a strong person and you *can* cope with your fear.

Information About Your Surroundings

When you board the plane in the summertime, the air coming into the plane is air conditioned. If humid conditions exist, you may see a gray vapor coming from the vents located just above your head along both sides of the plane. Many travelers mistake this vapor for smoke. It is not smoke. It is condensation from the air conditioner. The way to tell condensation from smoke is that condensation dissipates; smoke does not. Smoke stays in the air and becomes progressively thicker.

Next, locate the card in the seat-back pocket in front of you that tells the type of plane you are flying. This will be useful later as you try to identify the sounds the plane makes.

Five minutes before departure from the gate, you will hear a single chime when the captain illuminates the fasten seat belt sign. Soon after the chime, a flight attendant will ask you to fasten your seat belt.

The Flight Begins

During this stage of the flight, three events take place that are significant to the fearful flyer:

- Closing the door

- Departing the gate

- Starting the engines

Closing the Door

The flight will begin with an announcement from the ground crew thanking you for flying their airline. The door will then be shut and locked into place. You will hear the announcement, "Flight attendants, please prepare for departure" and a single chime. The shutting of the door is a difficult time for many fearful fliers because they feel that they cannot get off the plane once the door is locked. If this is a difficult time for you, do not sit and listen intently for the signal that the door is about to close. Work on your breathing and try to keep yourself as calm as possible.

Remind yourself that you chose to be on this flight because you know that you *can* handle air travel.

The announcement that the plane is about to depart not only lets the flight attendants know that the plane is about to leave the jet bridge, it is an instruction for them to arm the evacuation slides so that they will deploy automatically if an emergency evacuation is required.

Departing the Gate

The plane may depart from the jet bridge in one of two ways. If it is a narrow-body plane (one aisle), with its engines located in the tail (B-727; MD-80, F-100), it may *power back* or be pushed back. In a power back, the captain revs up the engines, moves the plane forward until it has moved off the flat spots that have developed in the tires, and then reverses the thrust of the engines by deploying the thrust reversers located at the rear of the engines. The plane moves in reverse under its own power.

Under certain circumstances, such as when there is a lot of equipment parked in the vicinity of the plane or there are workers present, a power back is not possible and the plane is pushed back by a heavy tractor. Wide-body planes and smaller jet planes that have the engines mounted under the wings (B-737) will always be pushed back. This is because the engines are so powerful that reversing them might create a wind that could damage the terminal or equipment in the area, or foreign material might be sucked into the engine and damage the engine. The only difference to you is that the push back will be very quiet, and the power back is likely to be quite noisy. Both are perfectly safe, perfectly normal.

Starting the Engines

The engine may be started just before departure from the jet bridge if the plane is to be powered back, or just after push back. In any event some unusual things happen that may scare you if you are not aware of why they happen.

The captain diverts air from a small jet engine called an auxiliary power unit (APU) to start the jet engines. Up until start time this jet engine has probably been used to provide air conditioning/heating and electricity to the plane. When engine start begins, you will notice the lights flicker because the power is interrupted momentarily. This may occur two or three times depending on how many engines your plane has.

This is perfectly normal and does not mean that there is a short in the electrical system.

When the air is diverted from the air-conditioning to the starter, the air that has been coming into the plane through the small vents (sometimes called *gaspers* or *eyeball vents*) will stop and so will the swishing sound of the air coming through the vents. Fresh air is still coming into the plane, but at a greatly reduced rate. Although this slowing of fresh air only lasts for two or three minutes, on a hot, muggy day the temperature inside the plane may rise a bit. If you are claustrophobic, the noticeable reduction of air flow and the rising temperature may activate your fear. Anticipate this event, remind yourself that fresh air is still coming into the plane, and concentrate on controlling your breathing.

Taxiing

Once the jet engines have begun and permission to taxi has been received by the pilot from ground control, the captain will begin to taxi. As you taxi toward the runway, four things will occur that may frighten you. One of these is that you will smell the acrid exhaust from other airplanes. The plane is not on fire! This occurs because planes take their air from outside, and if your plane is directly behind another plane you will get some of its exhaust. Rest assured that the captain smells the fumes just as you do and will eliminate the problem as quickly as possible.

You will also hear the grating and sometimes chattering of the huge disc brakes as the captain slows and stops during taxiing. While this awful sound would mean disaster if it occurred in your car, it is perfectly normal for airplanes. Incidentally, this sound will be decidedly worse if your plane landed a few minutes prior to your departure and the brakes have not had a chance to cool.

Safety Announcements

During taxi, the flight attendants also make the safety announcements. They tell you how to fasten and unfasten your seat belt, where the emergency exits are located, what to do with the oxygen mask in the case of depressurization, and how to use the flotation devices you will need if the plane makes a landing in water. They make this announcement on each flight because it is the law. You should pay close attention to these announcements, particularly those dealing with the emergency exits. The chances are extremely slight that you will ever have to use them, but if you do, you want to know where they are. The flight attendants are trained to empty a full plane in ninety seconds with half the exits blocked. You need to be ready to help by getting out of the plane if the need arises.

Extending the Flaps

The captain will extend the flaps on the wings on most planes during taxi. Two mechanical systems are used to deploy the flaps: hydraulic pumps and jackscrew and cables. Boeing planes, such as the B-767, and the McDonnell Douglas DC-10 have jackscrews, which are driven by hydraulic pumps. Planes designated by MD, which are newer McDonnell Douglas planes, have cable systems. When the flaps are deployed in Boeing-built planes or the DC-10, there is a high-pitched whine and the very noticeable mechanical sound of the jackscrews turning. The cable system is much quieter, and if you are sitting away from the wing, you may not hear the flaps being deployed. If you are sitting near the wing, the sound you hear when the flaps are deployed will be like a muffled groan. You need to be able to identify these sounds because you will hear them during taxi, after takeoff, during climb, several times during the descent, and after you land.

Please note that some planes do not deploy flaps prior to takeoff because the wing is so efficient it does not need the extra lift provided by flaps in many instances. The Fokker 100, a plane built in the Netherlands, is an example of such a plane. Don't panic if you do not see the flaps being extended on the wing of your aircraft.

Setback: A Ground Delay

One unpleasant and unexpected event that may occur just before takeoff is a ground delay. This occurs because air traffic control at your destination has determined that they must slow incoming traffic in order to avoid holding patterns. Ask yourself this question, "Would I rather hold on the ground before takeoff or in the air before I land?" Almost all fearful flyers would rather hold on the ground.

Holding, whether it is in the air or on the ground, is a problem for all flyers, but people who are claustrophobic have the most trouble. Why? Because they "psych" themselves up to take the flight, look at the scheduled flight time, and convince themselves that they can indeed breathe for one hour, albeit with difficulty. Then they get on the plane, taxi out, and hear this announcement, "Ladies and gentlemen we have been advised that we will be held on the ground for thirty minutes because of weather in the Dallas area." Suddenly, the one-hour flight is one and one-

half hours, and panic sets in. In one of my fearful flyer seminars this exact
scenario developed. Soon after the announcement, one of the participants
jumped up and ran from her coach class seat to first class, which is room-
ier. In about two minutes she returned to her seat and started to work on
controlling her breathing. She realized that if she could breathe for one
hour, she could breathe for two or more hours. She changed her irrational
thoughts.

The Takeoff Roll

Takeoff begins with a single announcement, "Flight attendants, prepare
for takeoff," and a single chime. Once this is done, the captain may make
either what is called a rolling take off, which means that the captain does
not stop after the plane rolls onto the runway, or a standing takeoff. Sometimes in a standing takeoff, the captain will set the brakes of the plane,
allow the engine to rev up, and then release the brakes. This will usually
occur on short runways (this does not mean they are dangerous) when
the plane is fully loaded. If you are flying out of La Guardia Airport in
New York, Orange County's John Wayne Airport in Santa Ana, California,
or St. Thomas in the Virgin Islands, you are likely to experience this type
of takeoff from time to time. It will also be used on very hot days in many
locations. This type of standing takeoff is used because it takes a jet engine
six to seven seconds to reach its maximum power, and the captain has
decided to allow this to occur to ensure a safe takeoff.

    Most takeoffs are standing takeoffs that involve a simple procedure:
the captain pushes the throttles forward to takeoff power, the plane moves
ahead slowly at first, then accelerates until it reaches the takeoff speed,
which is in the neighborhood of 150 miles per hour for most planes. During this *takeoff roll* you may hear a bump-bump-bump-bump as the nose
wheel of the plane passes over the lights that are embedded in the center
of the runway. Generally speaking, the captain will steer the plane to the
left or right of these lights and this noise will not last more than a few
seconds. You may also feel some substantial bumps as the plane passes
over expansion joints or rough places in the runway. These present no
greater safety problem than you experience when your car passes over
expansion joints or bumps on the highways.

    How long will the takeoff roll take? That depends upon the type of
plane, the weather conditions, and the load. I have timed many small jets
and commuters and the usual takeoff roll is approximately thirty-five seconds. A B-757, which has the highest power-to-weight ratio of any commercial plane, may take only twenty-five seconds to complete the takeoff

roll. A fully loaded B-747-400, which can weigh nearly one million pounds when fully loaded, may take twice as long or over a minute to get to the air speed it needs to fly.

Liftoff

The captain knows the exact speed needed for the plane to fly. This speed is precalculated based on the weight of the airplane, passengers, baggage, and weather conditions. So that this speed can be recognized easily, the captain places a small marker known as a bug on the air speed indicator. Once bug speed is reached, the captain pulls back on the yoke, the nose lifts, and the plane begins to fly. For most people, this is the scariest moment in the flight. If you are one of them, you must work very hard to control your breathing and your heart rate. Be ready to snap your rubber band and tell yourself to stop thinking those irrational thoughts if racing thoughts occur. Snap it repeatedly and with vigor if it becomes necessary. Then return immediately to controlling your breathing.

At the moment of liftoff you will here a thud as the weight is lifted from the landing gear. This occurs because the landing gear extends to its full limit in its housing. Within seconds his sound will be followed by the landing gear doors opening (thump), the landing gear coming up and being locked into placed (bump), and the landing gear doors closing (thump). This is a noisy time and can be quite disconcerting if you do not anticipate these sounds and identify them as they occur.

If you are sitting in the rear of the plane at the time of *rotation* (when the captain pulls back on the yoke to raise the nose and lift off) you may experience the sensation that the plane is falling. This is not the case, but if you are in the rear of the plane, you are actually descending for a split second. Why? At the time the nose of the plane comes up, the tail of the plane actually descends several feet; thus you feel that you are falling. Conversely, if you are sitting in the front of the plane at the time of rotation, you will have the sensation of rising, which you are. To help you visualize this experience, think of the plane as the teeter-totter or seesaw that you played on as a child. When one end goes up, the other end goes down.

Climb

The first thing you will hear during the climb is the sound of the flaps being retracted. This will typically occur in three stages as the plane accelerates. Listen for these sounds, and if you are sitting by a window and are not afraid of heights, verify that these are the sounds of the flaps by watching them move when the sound is occurring.

During the takeoff roll and at liftoff, the plane is at takeoff power. This is not unlike the situation you experience in your car when you are trying to get up enough speed to merge with the traffic on the freeway. As soon as you get into the traffic pattern, you lift your foot off the accelerator. After a few seconds into the climb, the captain reduces the power to *climb power* and lowers the nose of the aircraft to reduce the climb rate. This is done because the speed limit for an airplane below 10,000 feet is 281 miles per hour. If this is exceeded, the captain can be fined $10,000 or more. Slowing the climb rate also reduces engine wear and saves the airlines money in maintenance costs. However, this combination of actions produces the sensation of falling in many people.

Why does your body tell you that you are falling when you are in fact still climbing and accelerating? First, the noise in the airplane lessens, something you have always associated with slowing down. Second, because the nose is lowered, your stomach continues to climb for a split second, as it does when you go over a large incline on a roller coaster. The difference is that on the roller coaster you do in fact descend. In a plane your mind interprets what is happening to you incorrectly: it lies to you. When pilots are in training, they are taught to ignore their senses and their mind's interpretation of what is occurring in the plane and trust their instruments. Unfortunately, your seat is not equipped with an air speed indicator and an altimeter. You need to anticipate this first power reduction and the lowering of the nose and label it as it occurs by reminding yourself that the plane is not falling.

Turns and Level-Offs

You may experience one or more turns soon after the plane lifts off. These are often necessary because of noise abatement restrictions. I'm sure you can appreciate the fact that home owners do not want planes flying over their houses at low altitudes, so in order to accommodate them, planes are routed around populated areas. Planes turn when the captain simultaneously lowers one wing and raises the other using the ailerons. When the plane banks, many people feel as though it is going to keep on rolling and fall out of the sky. Some feel this so intensely that they lean to the right if the plane is banking to the left to "help" the plane remain stable. The plane is quite stable, and your body movements are unnecessary. Banks are restricted to 30 degrees and, under normal operating conditions, will be no greater than this. However, it may help you to know that the plane could in fact make a 360 degree roll (all the way around), level off, and fly quite nicely.

During the climb you may also experience intermediate level-offs, which may surprise you. These occur primarily in areas of heavy traffic, such as the New York/Newark area, Dallas/Fort Worth area, Chicago, Atlanta, Miami, and Los Angeles, but they can occur at any airport. You need to know that planes follow highways in the sky just as you follow highways on the ground. These highways are spaced 1,000 feet apart vertically, and level-offs are necessary to maintain the 1,000 feet of separation required for planes flying under 10,000 feet.

When a level-off occurs, the captain lowers the nose of the aircraft and pulls the throttle back. This produces sensations that are not unlike those associated with the reduction of power from takeoff to climb, but they are less pronounced. However, many fearful flyers interpret these level-offs as signs that something is wrong with the aircraft. This is not the case. They are normal procedures.

What the Chimes Mean

I have already alerted you to the fact that you will hear a single chime at departure and another at takeoff. In both instances these are signals from the flight deck to the flight attendants and are accompanied by verbal announcements. During the climb you will hear at least two chimes. One occurs at 1,500 feet to alert the flight attendants that they can begin their service. The second occurs at 10,000 feet. This alerts the flight attendants to announce that passengers may begin using devices that can interfere with navigational instruments (personal computers, tape players, CD players, and so on) and endanger the flight at lower altitudes.

When the plane descends, the captain will once again ring a chime at 10,000 feet (flight attendants will ask passengers to stow restricted devices) and at 1,500 feet. You may hear other chimes during the climb period as passengers request assistance by pushing the flight attendant's call button that is located either in the panel just above their heads or in their armrests.

By now you have determined that the chimes are a communication system between the pilots and the flight attendants, and between the passengers and the flight attendants. They also allow flight attendants in the front of the plane to communicate with those in the rear of the plane. When a chime sounds, flight attendants can recognize the source of the message by the color of a light that is illuminated in panels at both ends of the plane. Thus they know whether it comes from a passenger, another flight attendant, or from the captain.

Unless the chimes are associated with the events already described, such as departure, take-off, or passing through 1,500 and 10,000 feet, they can be interpreted as follows:

- One chime—call me when you have time

- Two chimes—call me as quickly as possible

- Three chimes—call me now

- Four chimes—come to the cockpit now

Four chimes are rarely heard and are used when something unusual is happening in the airplane. I heard four chimes once when was flying from Seattle to Raleigh-Durham and a drunken man fell, cut his head badly, and began bleeding profusely. Immediately thereafter, an announcement was made asking if there was a physician on board. One was located, the passenger was cared for, and we proceeded to our destination.

Four chimes are used in an emergency, and that is why you will hear it so rarely. I spoke personally with more than a dozen pilots who, together, have more than 200 years of flying experience, and not one of them had ever used four chimes. There is a time when you might hear four, or even more chimes, however. Children often discover the flight attendant's call buttons in the armrests and may ring them repeatedly.

Cruise

"Ladies and gentlemen, we have reached our cruising altitude of 35,000 feet, and we are expecting smooth air, so I will be turning the seat belt sign off at this time. Feel free to move about the cabin, but when you are in your seats please keep your seat belts fastened for your safety." This announcement alerts you to the fact that you have reached cruising altitude. You should comply with the request to keep your seat belt fastened because, as you now know, turbulence cannot be forecast. For this reason I also suggest that you steady yourself with one hand by keeping it on a seat if you walk about the cabin or visit the lavatory.

Several kinds of fears may occur during cruise. People who are afraid of heights are vulnerable. They may reject the idea that the air has mass and the plane is kept in the air because of the lift provided by the wings and sit anxiously, rigidly waiting for the plane to confirm their beliefs by falling out of the sky. Even the slightest bit of turbulence confirms their faulty hypothesis, and they react with panicky thoughts and an out-of-control body. If this is your problem, snap those thoughts away with your rubber band, control your breathing, and get back in touch with the rational side of your brain. You may want to use a mantra such as, "I'm safe, the plane cannot fall; I'm safe, the plane cannot fall; I'm safe, the plane cannot fall."

The person who is claustrophobic or who has panic attacks may become panicky because the pilot, along with telling you how high you are, may tell you how many hours and minutes it will be before you land. Enter the thoughts about being trapped, not having enough air, and having a heart attack and dying. Concentrate on your breathing for several minutes and then reconsider your irrational thoughts. The absolute worst thing that can happen is that you will hyperventilate and pass out. While this may be embarrassing, at least you will spend a portion of the trip in relative comfort (until you regain conciousness—only kidding, of course).

Take Time to Work on Your Fears

During cruise is the best time to work on your fears. Once you compose yourself, determine your SUDS score. Then, using the RED technique, the Valsalva maneuver, thought stopping, and muscle relaxation, try to lower your SUDS score by one number. If it is at eight, try to lower it to seven. When you get to seven, try to lower it to six, and so on. If you learn that you are in control of your thoughts and your physical reactions, you have taken a huge step toward eliminating your fear. If you feel as if your fear is under control, systematically look at all the things you are afraid of as you cruise: invite your fear to fly with you.

Under no circumstances should you suppress your fear during this phase of your recovery. Don't play loud music, talk incessantly to the person sitting next to you, or distract yourself with crossword puzzles. Attend to your fearful thoughts and the physical reactions to them. Learn that you can control them.

If your fearful thoughts do not subside with the strategies outlined earlier (RED technique, Valsalva maneuver, and so on.) you may want to try a strategy discussed in Chapter 7: worry time. This begins by identifying the intrusive thoughts that are scaring you, noting the time on your watch (yes, you'll need it now), and then concentrating on repeating to yourself the worrisome thought as often as you can in five minutes. While this seems like a risky approach on the surface, most fearful flyers cannot engage in this technique for five minutes without realizing how silly their thoughts are and discontinuing their worrying. However, if this strategy increases your panicky thoughts, discontinue it and return to controlling your breathing.

If you find that you are relaxing a bit, but cannot get comfortable because you are still "flying the plane" by looking out the window, listening to every noise, and monitoring the flight attendants' faces for signs of panic, you may also want to use a version of worry time. Repeat over and over, "I must monitor every phase of this flight or the plane will crash." As you do this, switch systematically from monitoring the wings to see if they are still attached, to listening to the engines to make sure that they are still running, to the flight attendants' faces to make sure they are still calm. Do this until you are absolutely sick of it.

Turbulence

The word *turbulence* strikes terror in the hearts of most fearful flyers, particularly those who are afraid of heights (falling) or have concern about the stability and mechanical integrity (the wings falling off) of the aircraft. Turbulence can occur at any phase of the flight, but seems to cause the greatest problem for people during cruise, perhaps because this phase of the flight may last longer.

Measuring Turbulence

Pilots measure turbulence on a scale of zero to six. On every flight plan there is a turbulence index, which is an estimate of the turbulence along the route. This index is determined partially by looking at weather and partially by reports from pilots who have already flown the route earlier in the day. A zero on the turbulence index (TI) indicates that no turbulence or very light turbulence is expected, and a six indicates very heavy turbulence. Planes are not dispatched into areas where heavy turbulence is expected (TI=6), and so far as possible, moderate turbulence is avoided by taking alternate routes. Why? Is turbulence dangerous? No! Dispatchers and pilots want you to have the most comfortable ride possible and will take alternate routes that may cause schedule delays to make sure this happens.

How can you measure turbulence? Order a glass of water that is filled almost full. If the TI is zero or one, the water will barely move. As the TI approaches two, the water will begin to move, and as it approaches four, it will spill, sometimes in substantial quantities. When the flight attendants pick up cups and dishes because of turbulence, they are expecting something greater than a one or two. They are doing this so things will not spill on you, not because the plane will fall out of the sky and they want to look neat after the crash (I'm kidding, of course). Also, when the captain asks the flight attendants to take their seats, he is doing so to prevent injury, not because the plane is in danger.

Dealing with Turbulence

What should you do during turbulence? Do *not* use your rubber band to stop your thoughts. The palm of your hand will become quite sore very quickly. Also, do *not* become rigid, hang on to the armrests for dear life, and place your foot against the seat support in front of you. *Do* fasten your seat belt tightly, because this will increase your feeling of security, and then assume the *jello position.* You assume the jello position by relaxing any muscles that are particularly tense, putting your hands loosely at your sides or on the armrests, and pretending that you are a mold of jello quivering with the rhythm induced by the turbulence. In other words, you try to be totally relaxed and move with the plane.

Moving in response to the plane can be done either with music or without it. My wife Sandra plays her tape of Jerry Lee Lewis's "Whole Lot of Shaking Going On" and moves in rhythm with the music. This helps to remind her that, while the plane may shake in turbulence, it is not a dangerous phenomenon (just a whole lot of shaking). You may wish to choose some other music or simply move with the rhythm of the turbulence when it occurs. Will you look stupid if you "dance" with the rhythm of turbulence? To quote Forrest Gump, "Stupid is as stupid does." How can it be stupid to deal with your fear?

Finally, an extremely effective way to deal with the fear that develops during turbulence is to repeat a mantra that reminds you that turbulence is not a safety issue. Two that I recommend are, "it's a comfort issue" or "it's a service issue." By repeating these sayings, you are reminded that turbulence is not a safety issue even though it is not comfortable; or that, while turbulence may disrupt the service and you may not get your meal or your drink, it will not knock the plane from the sky.

Descent

The descent is the favorite part of the flight for most people, including fearful flyers. Perhaps the first thing that will cue you that the descent has begun is reduced engine noise. In fact, the engines are pulled back to idle for much of the descent, and the plane is actually gliding. The captain never shuts the engines off.

If you are extremely sensitive to the movement of the plane, you may also notice that the captain has lowered the nose of the aircraft. One sure cue that the descent has begun is that you begin to develop a stuffy feeling in your ear. As the cabin pressure is lowered, a disequilibrium among the pressure in your outer, middle, and inner ear develops. Swallowing hard or yawning will equalize this pressure in most instances—so will pinching your nose and blowing as though you are blowing into a handkerchief. Begin by blowing gently, gradually increasing the pressure until you can hear properly.

You may experience an *expedited descent*. This occurs when air traffic control wants the plane at an altitude that it could not attain using typical approaches. What happens is that the captain deploys the *spoilers* or speed brakes, which are boardlike structures on the wing, and they pop up into the air passing over the wing. This "spoils" the lift, and the plane descends more rapidly. Some planes, such as the DC-10, vibrate a bit when the spoilers are deployed. If you suspect that spoilers have been deployed, look out the window (if you are not afraid of heights) to verify this. The spoilers are near the leading edge of the wing and begin about one-third of the way down the wing. They are several feet long and, as noted above, are shaped like a board.

An unexpected event that can occur during descent is that your plane will be put into a holding pattern. As noted earlier, most delays occur on the ground prior to takeoff. Occasionally you will be nearing your destination and air traffic control will determine that it is not safe to have all inbound traffic continue. They will ask the captain to enter a holding pattern, which is nothing more than flying in circles or flying *vectors* (a zigzag pattern, as opposed to a straight line).

In addition to the idea of being in the sky longer, which can produce fearful thoughts, you may become alarmed if you look out the window and see other planes that seem to be quite near flying the same pattern as your plane. In the circular holding pattern, planes are stacked at 1,000-foot intervals and are in no danger of colliding. If you get panicky, snap your rubber band, control your breathing, and remind yourself of two facts: all the planes in the stack are being observed via air traffic control radar, and your plane is equipped with a traffic and collision avoidance system to prevent midair collisions. Incidentally, the plane at the lowest altitude will land first, and then other planes descend 1,000 feet on the next circle, and another plane lands, and this continues until all the planes are safely down.

During descent there are likely to be several intermediate level-offs, just as there were during the climb. When this happens, the nose of the plane will come up and the engines will be returned to cruise power. Many people mistakenly believe that the plane is starting to climb again when this occurs. At 10,000 feet you will hear a single chime. This will be repeated at 1,500 feet. You will also hear the flaps deployed several times (perhaps as many as five times) during the descent.

Wallowing, Crosswinds, and Rejected Landings

There are several things that occur during the final phase of the flight that may scare you. One of these is that the plane "wallows," or rocks back and forth. This does not mean that the plane is out of control. The control surfaces of the wing are more sensitive at slower speeds and reduced power and this produces this movement. Also, the captain is making minor corrections to ensure that the plane will land in exactly the right location on the runway.

If you are looking out the window from the rear, you may observe that the plane appears to be flying "at an angle" instead of straight toward the runway. Whenever the plane is landing into a crosswind, the captain puts it into a "crab," and while the center of the plane is flying toward the center of the runway, the nose of the plane is not pointed directly at the runway. The crab is removed just before touchdown, the wing pointing toward the crosswind is lowered, and the plane touches down on one wheel, quickly followed by the other. This is the classic crosswind landing, which is performed safely hundreds of times each day.

Perhaps the scariest thing that can occur during descent is when the landing is rejected and the pilot performs what is known as a go-around. This typically occurs because there is another plane on the runway. It is illegal for the captain to land with another plane anywhere on the runway. This can also occur because weather conditions change (for example, a crosswind picks up to the point of being unsafe, or because the pilot feels that he cannot land safely for other reasons). One pilot rejected a landing at Raleigh-Durham Airport because a deer was on the runway.

When a landing is rejected, you are typically on final approach and the landing gear has been lowered. Suddenly, the power comes up, the landing gear is retracted, and the plane begins to climb. What you should know is that for every landing there is a plan for a rejected landing, and that at every airport, certain air space is reserved for rejected landings. Even though a rejected landing is startling and may be scary, it is perfectly safe.

If a normal landing is to occur, the landing gear is lowered with a thump, bump, thump a few hundred feet above the ground; the nose and power come up (remember, modern jetliners and commuters land on their rear wheels first); and you touch down.

Taxi In

At touchdown, the reversers are deployed to reverse the thrust of the engines and provide braking action. Also, the speed brakes or spoilers on the wings come up automatically, to reduce the lift the wing is providing so that the weight of the airplane is on the wheels. Then as the plane slows, the brakes are used to slow it further. The brakes are extremely powerful, and you will move forward in your seat when they are applied. You will also hear them screech and grind as they take hold. Within a few seconds, the captain will turn the plane off the runway, retract the flaps, which were fully extended at landing, and taxi to the gate. You will be advised to remain in your seats until the plane is safely parked at the gate by an announcement from the flight deck. (Please follow this advice no matter how badly you want to get out.) Finally, the seat belt sign will go off, the door will open and you will deplane.

All you need to do at this point in the flight is congratulate yourself on flying. If you are a perfectionist, you may begin to criticize yourself for not functioning as well as you "should have" on the plane. Use your rubber band to snap away these irrational thoughts and congratulate yourself on your accomplishment.

Summary

A successful flight begins when you make your reservations and continues through until the doors open and you deplane. You must take charge of arrangements before the flight and take control of your fear during the flight. The keys to controlling your fear are understanding the techniques that you will use to control your thoughts and physical responses and using them at the time the fearful response comes.

9

Developing Your Own Flight Plan

Preparation and information are the keys to a successful flight. Chapters 5 and 6 give you the best available information about airplanes, personnel, and the industry in general. The bottom line must be that, while flying is not perfect, it is safer than alternative modes of transportation. Throughout this book you have also been given specific techniques for coping with your physical and mental reactions to your fear. Now it is time to prepare for your next stage, your graduation from fearful flyer to confident flyer. Chapter 8 took you through a dress rehearsal of your first successful flight. Now, I want you to engage in the final stages of preparation for the flight.

Making the Reservation

Before you make your reservation, lay out a master plan that involves flying several times if at all possible. Once you have taken your first flight, you need to fly again soon, preferably within three months, and sooner is better. All too often I have seen people who did not fly within a few months of their first flight begin to doubt their ability to be successful again, and then have their fear return. Don't let this happen to you.

Length of the Flight

I want you to be in control of every step in the preparation for your next flight, and this includes making the reservation. Decide on the length of flight you wish to take, and whether the flight is to be for business or pleasure. I recommend that you schedule the flight for the business of facing your fear of flying and the pleasure of leaving it behind. By this I mean that, ideally, your only objective on your graduation flight should be to work on eliminating your fear of flying. If it is a business trip or a family vacation, other issues, such as keeping up appearances in front of colleagues or watching your children, may keep you from concentrating on your fear.

If you live on either coast, there are numerous, relatively short flights available to you. Many airlines offer shuttle services, such as those between New York and Boston and Los Angeles to San Francisco. These flights may take off every hour or so, and they last from forty-five minutes to an hour. You could, for example, fly to Boston or San Francisco for lunch in the morning and return that same afternoon.

I recommend that you make this flight a short one, by which I mean forty-five minutes to an hour in the air. Published airline schedules give the time from gate to gate. A flight that is scheduled to depart at 1:00 P.M. and arrive at 2:00 P.M. will be in the air about forty-five minutes. The remainder of the time will be spent backing away from the jet bridge, taxiing, or waiting. I recommend short flights because they have one distinct advantage: if you cannot reboard the plane, you can always rent a car or take the train back to your point of origin in a reasonable amount of time. Over 3,000 flyers boarded our graduation flights when the American Airlines fearful flyer program was operating. Only 2 elected not to take the return flight, but almost all fearful flyers who boarded those flights had some fear that they would be unable to make the return trip. If you schedule a short flight, the fear of being unable to get back on the plane after the first leg of your flight is minimized.

Other advantages of short flights are that they cost less and there is no need to take luggage. Also, if you schedule your flight on Saturday, there is likely to be less traffic congestion in the parking areas, fewer people in the airport, and fewer people on the plane because fewer people fly on Saturday than any other day. Flights on Sunday afternoon, Monday, and Friday are likely to be the most crowded because these are peak travel periods.

A Day or Night Flight?

In addition to deciding whether to take a short, intermediate, or long flight you should consider whether you wish to fly during the day or night. Some fearful flyers prefer to fly during the day so they can watch the ground. Others prefer flying at night because the darkness makes them less aware of the height of the airplane. From a safety viewpoint, it makes no difference whether you fly at night or during the day. If you have concerns about the time of day you fly, take those into consideration on this flight. However, your goal should be to fly comfortably at night or during the day.

What Type of Plane?

You may also wish to select the type of plane you fly. Airplanes come in two general configurations; narrow bodies, which have one aisle, and wide-bodies, which have two aisles. Delta flies Lockheed-built L-1011s, the McDonnell Douglas MD-11s, and the Boeing B-767, which are all wide-bodies. American also flies the MD-11 and the B-767, as well as the McDonnell Douglas DC-10. United, Northwest, and TWA fly wide-bodies built by Boeing, the B-747. United and other airlines will soon be flying the B-777, which is a wide-body. The McDonnell Douglas DC-9-80 is a popular narrow-body plane, as is the older Boeing B-727. If you take a short trip in the United States, you are likely to be on a narrow-body plane and when flying internationally, you will probably be on a wide-body.

People with claustrophobia almost always prefer wide-bodies because of their spaciousness. Some people who have had or are having panic attacks also prefer wide-bodies because they can get up and move about during the flight. Also, because turbulence is a bit less noticeable on large planes, some fearful flyers who are particularly concerned about this issue prefer wide-bodies. If you take my recommendation and take a short flight, unfortunately, you will have few choices about the type of plane you fly. If you fly across the United States, to the Caribbean, to Mexico, or to Canada, you may have options. Just check with the reservation agent at the time you make your reservation.

Choosing Your Seat

When you are making your reservation, you should choose your seat if possible. (Some of the low-cost airlines such as Southwest do not make preflight seat assignments.) Where should you sit? That depends upon a variety of factors, not the least of which is the nature of your problem. The cabins of most aircrafts are divided into two sections, first class and coach class; although some planes have a third section, business class. First class costs two to eight times the coach class fare depending on the length of the trip. Business class costs two to four times as much as coach class in some instances, and affords you more room, more comfortable seats, and better service. Both first and business class are in the front of the airplane and are quieter.

Many claustrophobics can fly in moderate comfort in first and business class because of the extra space. They, and people who have had or now have panic attacks, feel less "trapped" in business and first class. You must decide if the extra money is worth the extra comfort. You should also be thinking long term. Will you normally be flying in coach class in the future? If yes, you should probably be flying in coach class on your graduation flight.

Coach class also has some seating areas that you should consider. One of these is called *bulkhead*, which is the row of seats behind first class, just behind the partition that divides coach and first class. Another is *exit row* seats, which are the seats beside the emergency exits. Consider selecting bulkhead seats if you are claustrophobic, or have had or now have panic attacks, because you have more personal space. Exit row seats also provide additional space, typically about twenty inches more, which is an obvious advantage if you are concerned about feeling closed in. In most instances you cannot preselect exit row seats, but you can ask if they are available when you arrive at the airport. If you are disabled or carrying a small child, or cannot remove the airplane exit door in an emergency, you will not be allowed to sit in these seats, however.

Typically, airplanes have aisle, middle, and window seats in the coach class area. Most people who suffer from claustrophobia and people who have had or are now having panic attacks prefer aisle seats because they feel less confined. In aisle seats, they are not packed between two or more people, as they are in a middle seat, and because there is no luggage compartment overhead, they have more space over their heads and to their sides. In a bit of a paradox, some people who are claustrophobic prefer to sit by the window and look out because this gives them the illusion of space. If you are claustrophobic and have the opportunity to board a stationary plane, try both aisle and window seats to see which works best for you.

I recommend a window seat if you are afraid of heights and are not claustrophobic. If you sit by the window, you can lower the plastic shade, thus controlling your visual space. Probably the second best place for you to sit if you are afraid of heights is on the aisle. Your objective should be not to look out of the plane until it starts its descent. Then, you should look out of the plane only when you are lower than 1,500 feet. (Quiz: how will you know when you are lower than 1,500 feet? See Appendix A for the answer if you do not know it already.)

Finally, if you have a choice between sitting in the tail of the coach class section or toward the front, choose the front. This is particularly true if you are concerned about turbulence and the noises in the aircraft, or if you are claustrophobic. The tail of the plane tends to move a bit more than other, more stable portions of the plane, and bounce a bit more in turbulence. Also, in the tail you are sitting either behind the engines (if they are under the wing) or just ahead of them (if they are mounted in the tail), and you will be able to hear every change in engine noise, which can be quite disconcerting. Remember, the most stable portion of the plane is over the wings. However, this is also one of the noisiest sections because much of the machinery that operates the plane is located under the wing area.

Choosing Support Persons

A question many people ask is, "Should I fly with another person?" Generally, yes, but there are some factors to consider. One of these is whether you know a person who can fly with you who will be 100 percent supportive, regardless of your behavior. The last thing you need is to be worrying about whether your behavior will be approved by the people around you, particularly the person who is supposed to be supporting you. A support person, if properly briefed, can help you use your flight plan and make the entire experience more bearable. Support people can also be rich sources of pleasant memories as you reflect on your victory.

Generally, I suggest that you not fly with your spouse, parents, or children. If you get frightened before the flight, people who love you are likely to give you permission to avoid the flight because they see the pain you are in. Unfortunately, having someone say, "You don't have to do this today" may be all the reason you need to avoid the flight. Life-long friends and nonjudgmental relatives provide the best support.

Setting Goals

As strange as it may seem, setting goals for the flight when you will confront your fear will probably be difficult. Before I go into this topic in detail, take a few minutes to think about your last flight. Consider each phase of the flight: taxi, takeoff, cruise, and landing. How frightened were you at each of these stages?

Using your SUDS score (1 = completely relaxed to 10 = totally scared) rate your fear at each of these steps on the chart below. Also, write out other problems you experienced, such as sweaty palms, tense muscles, and light-headedness during the flight.

Rating Your Last Flight

Stages of the Flight	SUDS Score
Taxi	_____
Takeoff	_____
Cruise	_____
Landing	_____
Other problems	_____

_____

_____

After you have thought about how scared you were and how you reacted to your fear, begin to reconsider your goals for your own graduation flight. Do *not* expect to function perfectly on this flight. One of the saddest moments experienced in working with fearful flyers was when people who had made tremendous advances against their fear declared privately, and then publicly, that they had failed. Failed? When they had gotten on a plane for the first time in years? Failed, when they had flown alcohol or drug free for the first time? Failed, when they only grabbed the seat once as the plane encountered some bumpy air instead on for dear life throughout the flight? Yes, some people count themselves as failures when they do not fly perfectly. Don't let yourself fall into this terrible trap.

Consider now what your goal for the next flight will be. Perhaps, instead of holding on in sheer terror, your goal should be to deal with the fear you experience on takeoff and reduce your SUDS score from 10 to 7. Perhaps it should be to rock and roll with the turbulence and remind yourself that turbulence is not a safety issue. Perhaps it should be to close the shade and remind yourself that planes cannot fall. You may even want to check the wings once in a while, because, if you recall the lesson on aerodynamics, planes cannot fall like a brick if the wings are attached. What follows are some sample goals:

- To reduce my SUDS score by three points during the takeoff roll and actual takeoff by controlling my physical responses to the fear.

- To move with the turbulence and remind myself, "It's a comfort issue, not a safety issue"

- To take a flight sober and to control my responses rather than letting them control me.

- To take a flight without checking the weather channel for thunderstorms.

- To get on the plane and fly and to work on my responses using my flight plan.

Take some time at this point to set a goal or goal for your next flight, and write them down in the space provided on the next page.

Goals for My Flight from Fear

_____

_____

_____

_____

_____

_____

Choosing Your Weapons Against Fear

In Chapter 4 I outlined several techniques for controlling various reactions to your fear, including breathing, thought-stopping strategies, an approach to relaxing tense muscles, and the Valsalva maneuver to slow a racing heart. You will need some or all of these techniques in your flight plan. What follows are my recommendations for the approach you should use on the plane. As you will see, these vary to some degree by problem type.

Weapons Against Fear of Crashing and Dying and Acrophobia

Recurrent, sometimes racing, thoughts that something absolutely catastrophic is about to happen to the plane and kill you and everyone else drive the fear of crashing or falling. Your first line of defense should probably be thought stopping. This means that you need to put a thick rubber band over your palm when you fly, be ready to yell "Stop" (your injunction), and use your positive self-statement. Thought stopping should be followed by controlling your breathing to calm yourself down and then muscle relaxation to relieve tension.

Once you have calmed down, use the sights, sounds, and sensations outline (Appendix A) to follow the progress of the flight and reassure yourself that the flight is proceeding normally. If concerns about turbulence are a part of your fear, you also need to include in your flight plan the idea of moving or dancing when turbulence occurs. Do *not* use thought stopping to control your response to turbulence, except as a last resort. Why? Because you need to snap your rubber band with vigor (it has to hurt) if it is to be effective, and you can literally pulverize your palm if the turbulence lasts several minutes.

You may also want to consider other things to do before and during the flight. For example, you may want to stick your head into the cockpit and meet the pilot. Many fearful flyers feel better if they can look into the eyes of the pilot. It is probably better not to tell him or her that you are afraid because some smart-aleck pilot may respond by telling you that he is also afraid. Please do not insult the crew, as one fearful flyer did, by asking them if they have been drinking. It is certainly okay to ask them questions about turbulence and weather en route, as well as whether they expect the flight to be on time. You may also wish to meet the flight attendant in the area where you are sitting and confide that you are a "nervous flyer." This provides you with a link to the crew, which some people find reassuring.

Here is a sample flight plan if you have a fear of falling or crashing:

When I Board the Plane

1. Greet the pilot.

2. Meet the flight attendant.

3. Close the blind covering the window.

If the Fear Comes

1. Use thought stopping:

   - Snap rubber band.

   - (To myself) yell, "Stop!"

   - Use a positive self-statement, "I can do this!"

2. Control breathing (five to seven minutes).

3. Relax breathing muscles if light-headedness persists.

If Turbulence Comes

1. Move, don't hang on.

2. Repeat this mantra, "This is not a safety issue. It only makes me uncomfortable."

3. Check the wings. "If they are still attached, I'm okay."

Weapons Against Claustrophobia

Claustrophobia is driven by recurring thoughts that you will run out of air and suffocate. The tightness in the throat and chest you feel when your breathing becomes quick and shallow heightens the fear and increases your racing thoughts. Your flight plan should begin with controlling your breathing. If you still get a bit light-headed after five minutes, you will want to focus on relaxing the muscles in the throat, chest, and abdomen. Use thought stopping only if you feel as if you are losing control of your body. I also recommend that you either take a small container of ice in an insulated bag or ask the flight attendant to bring you a glass of ice after you are seated. Ice on the tongue can make you feel much cooler.

For claustrophobia, consider boarding the plane just before takeoff (remember to check in so they do not give your seat to someone else). Never enter the jet bridge when it is crowded, particularly on a warm day. Once you are in your seat, turn on the small "eyeball" vent above your head and direct the flow of air onto your face. Remember, when you begin to feel warm, your fear can be heightened.

Here is a sample flight plan for claustrophobia:

When I Board the Plane

1. Board last.

2. Do not enter a crowded jet bridge.

3. Turn the air onto my face.

If the Fear Comes

1. Control my breathing (five to seven minutes).

2. If light-headedness persists, relax breathing muscles.

If Panic Comes

1. Use Thought stopping:

   • Snap rubber band.

   • Yell, "Stop" (to myself).

   • Use a positive self-statement, "I can control my breathing!"

2. Return to controlling my breathing.

Weapons Against Fear of Panic Attacks

Thoughts such as, I will have a panic attack and die, I will embarrass myself, or I will lose my mind and end up in a comatose state contribute to the fear of panic attacks. This fear is sometimes accompanied by concerns about having a heart attack. Your flight plan should begin by relaxing tense muscles that can alter the breathing process (throat, chest, and abdomen), followed by controlling your breathing.

You may also include the Valsalva maneuver if you are afraid that you will have a heart attack and have consulted your doctor about your cardiovascular health. Remember, the Valsalva maneuver must be followed by controlling your breathing for five to seven minutes if it is to be effective.

Here is a sample flight plan if you fear panic attacks:

When I Board the Plane

1. Remind myself, "I'm in control."

2. Turn air onto face.

3. Relax tense muscles.

If the Fear Comes

1. Control breathing (five to seven minutes).

2. If light-headedness persists, relax muscles that control the breathing process.

If Panic Comes

1. Use thought Stopping:

    • Snap rubber band.

    • Yell, "Stop" (to myself).

    • Use a Positive self-statement, "I'm in control of my body."

The three flight plans given in this section are only samples. By now you should understand your thoughts and physical responses to them. When you board the flight, have your own flight plan ready that is geared to your particular concerns. Why? You may recall the discussion of what happens to your brain when you become afraid: you cannot access information that has been stored in the brain. Leave nothing to chance. Develop your own flight plan on the form provided in Appendix C, laminate it, and when you board the plane, put it in your lap so you can consult it at any time during the flight.

Things to Do Before the Flight

Before you actually take your graduation flight, make several practice runs to the airport, particularly if you are concerned about driving and crowded places. Decide where you will park and where you will check your baggage (if you will have baggage with you). There are generally two places where baggage can be checked; curb side and in the terminal. I recommend curb side check-in if you already have your tickets.

If you are driving to the airport, there are usually three places to park: short-term lots, long-term lots, and off-site lots. Typically, the cost of parking is directly related to proximity to the airport. At some airports short-term parking can cost thirty dollars per day or more. Some fearful flyers who have not planned ahead have accidentally parked in short-term parking only to find after they return from their trip that parking cost more than their airline ticket.

After you reach the terminal during your practice run, pass through security to familiarize yourself with that operation and then go to the boarding area. Watch several flights board, then go to an area where you can watch takeoffs and landings. Watch several of these on each visit. If you have time, visit the tower on one of these trips, and try to visit a stationary aircraft.

If you have decided which airline you are going to fly, go to their passenger service office and ask for a tour. They are normally happy to accommodate you, and they are more likely to arrange a tour if you tell them you are a nervous flyer. If you are able to visit a stationary plane and the crew is on board, tell them you are a fearful flyer. My guess is that you will get more attention than you can imagine, if they are not preparing for another flight. Spend as much time on the plane as possible, particularly if the act of boarding the stationary plane increases your fear. The ultimate experience is getting a tour of the cockpit. A pilot can quickly demystify that intimidating environment, and an orientation to the safety features of the aircraft can do much to allay your fear. If the crew is on board and not busy, ask for a quick look at the cockpit.

Using Guided Imageries

In a very real sense the conquest of your fear begins with your imagination. I was conducting a seminar and one of the participants was not present on the second day, which was a Sunday. Since this was not unusual, I thought little about it. She arrived an hour late and confided that she had been to church to pray for help in her struggle. Just as she was leaving the church, a teenager came in wearing a tee shirt with the following saying on it: If You Can Imagine It, You Can Do It. Were her prayers answered? I cannot say, but I do know that she flew, and flew well. I also know that the words on that tee shirt are absolutely true. The first step in having a successful flight is to imagine yourself being victorious over your fear. If you can imagine yourself flying without fear, you can do it.

The fear of flying is unlike any other fear in one regard: you cannot take part of a flight. The USAir program for fearful flyers provides participants with an opportunity to taxi in an aircraft, which is quite helpful. The KLM (Royal Dutch Airlines) program uses flight simulators, which is an excellent idea. However, ultimately, you must take off and fly. Prior to this experience you can and should take imaginary flights. These will evoke all the mental and physical responses that you get on a real flight and allow you to practice dealing with your fear in a comfortable environment.

If you have anticipatory anxiety and have made a reservation to fly, you probably are already taking imaginary flights. In most (probably all) instances these imaginary flights are failures because they end in disaster. Disastrous imaginary flights only reinforce the fear and add to your suffering. These flights must be replaced with successful imaginary flights.

Before taking your first imaginary flight, make at least one practice trip to the airport so that the sights and sounds of the trip and the airport are familiar to you. Also, make your reservation so that you know your destination. In addition, it will be helpful if you know the type of plane you are flying and can visualize both the exterior and the interior of it.

Writing Out Your Self-Guided Imagery

Before you actually embark on preparing for your imaginary flight, make an outline of what you want to imagine, for example:

1. Leaving the house (plenty of time to get to the airport)

2. Trip to the airport (landmarks that I will see)

3. Parking (alternative if lot is full)

4. Entering the airport (sights and sounds)

5. Passing through security (sights and sounds)

6. Gate area (sights and sounds; my flight plan)

7. Boarding (sights and sounds; my flight plan)

8. Push back and taxi (sights, smells, and sounds; my flight plan)

9. Takeoff (sensations and sounds; my flight plan)

10. Cruise (sights, sensations, and sounds; my flight plan)

11. Turbulence (sensations; my flight plan)

12. Descent and landing (sights, sounds, and sensations; my flight plan)

The idea is to imagine each aspect of the flight, your reaction to it, and your coping response to the fear that may arise as your flight progresses. The following self-guided imagery can serve as a model for your own imagery.

> My luggage is in the car. I make a last-minute check of my apartment, lock the door, and get into my car. I start the car, back out of my parking spot, and pull onto the street. I pass the ugly purple chicken sign, then enter the freeway at the 14th Street on-ramp, and the traffic is light as it always is early in the morning. As I drive to the airport, I see a plane rise into the sky and my fear rises. I snap my rubber band and yell "Stop!" I can handle air travel.
>
> Twenty minutes after I leave home, I pull into the long-term parking lot, park my car, and catch the shuttle to the terminal with my carry-on luggage. I leave the shuttle, enter the airport, move through security, where the sounds of the metal detectors keep going off, and move quickly to the gate area. Several people have already arrived at the gate area, and because I am a bit early, I continue to walk down the concourse to ease the tension that is beginning to build. As I return, I hear the announcement, "Ladies and gentlemen, we will be boarding our Chicago flight by row numbers today." I check in, but I wait to board the plane until the final call for passenger boarding.
>
> After the announcement, "Ladies and gentlemen, all passengers holding tickets on this flight should be on board at this time." I enter the jet bridge, which is quite warm. I move quickly to the plane, step on, turn, pass through first class, and find my seat and stow my luggage in the overhead compartment. I take my seat, fasten the seat belt, and turn the vent over my head onto my face.
>
> I hear the announcement, "Flight attendants, please prepare for departure." Because the tension is rising, I work on calming my breathing using the skills I have learned. I begin to feel the tension subside, and I remind myself that there is plenty of air in the cabin. The flight attendants make the safety announcements, and I look around and locate the emergency exits.

The announcement, "Flight attendants, prepare for take-off," and a single chime indicate that we are ready to go. Engine noise comes up and we start to roll. In less than forty-five seconds we lift off with a thud as the wheels hit the end of the struts. Immediately, I hear the bump, thump, bump of the landing gear and the high-pitched sounds of the hydraulic pumps as the devices on the wings are retracted. I remind myself that these sounds are perfectly normal.

The captain lowers, lowers the nose and pulls back on the power. There is that feeling in the pit of my stomach I hate. I concentrate on slowing my breathing and remind myself that we are still climbing. I hear a single chime as we pass through 1,500 feet and another as we pass through 10,000 feet. The plane bumps a bit as we encounter some choppy air. I remind myself that turbulence is only a comfort issue, not a safety issue.

I hear a single chime and the pilot announces that they are expecting a smooth flight, but asks, "Please keep your seat belt fastened when in your seats." People get out of their seats, and the flight attendants start to serve beverages and snacks. The plane bumps a bit as we encounter some bumpy air, and the seat belt sign comes on. Suddenly the bumps are closer together. I turn on my CD player and start to move with the turbulence. I repeat, "It's a comfort issue. It's a comfort issue. It's a comfort issue," over and over again.

The noise outside the plane has lessened and we are definitely descending. The pressure in my ears builds, and I swallow hard to relieve it. The captain thanks us for flying his airline and reminds us that the seat belt sign is on and our seat belts should be fastened. I swallow again to relieve the pressure. I hear the hydraulic pumps again, then again. We are definitely approaching the airport. I work on controlling my breathing because I can feel the fear rising.

The whine of hydraulic pumps and the thump, bump, thump of the landing gear coming down signals that we are about to land. I'm excited! I've done it and better than I expected. I can fly! We touch down with a thump, engine noise comes up, brakes squeak and grind, and we turn off the runway. We taxi quickly to the gate. I hear the announcement, "Please stay in your seats until we are parked safely at the gate," followed by, "Flight attendants, please prepare for arrival." The plane stops, the doors open, and I deplane. It feels so-o-o-o good.

Write your imagery with your own problems in mind. It may vary significantly from the one you just read. Two things are important. First, take a complete flight and imagine those parts of the flight that will be difficult for you. Second, actually use the skills in your flight plan to cope with the reactions that you have. This means that you should review your flight plan before each imagery, place a rubber band over your palm, and be prepared to slow your racing heart or to relax your tense muscles.

At this time write out the self-guided imagery that you will use to practice for your graduation flight. Use a notebook or a computer or type-writer—whatever is most convenient—and call it: "My Successful Flight Imagery."

Putting Your Self-Guided Imagery into Practice

After you have written your imagery, you may wish to record it and play it as you practice. The recording can be used to cue the visual images that you experience. The practice sessions can occur anywhere so long as you will be undisturbed during them. Prior to the imagery, take several deep breaths, and then let the air out of your lungs as slowly as possible. Tense and relax any areas where you have muscle tension to make your-self as comfortable as possible. Once you are relaxed, run the "visual tape" of your imagery. After each session assess how you did using the follow-ing scale:

    1 = did not cope well at all
    5 = coped better than I have on airplanes in the past
    10 = coped very well

If you find that you are not coping satisfactorily with your imagi-nary flight, review the skills discussed in Chapter Four to make sure you are using them properly. If you are, keep practicing. You may also wish to review your information base. Sometimes one nagging thought, such as the air traffic control system is unsafe, can keep you from moving for-ward. If you have doubts, find a pilot, air traffic controller, or other expert to chat with about your concern. I have received dozens of calls from people who just wanted to clarify some minor point and they felt I was a credible source. Once the minor points were cleared up, they could con-tinue and confront their fear.

Finally, there is no formula for how many imageries you will need to complete. I suggest that you practice once a day for at least two weeks before your flight. Use self-guided imageries in conjunction with strategies for dealing with anticipatory anxiety if that is one of your problems. They are not a substitute for them.

Packing a Comfort Kit

Whether or not you are taking luggage on your trip, you should pack the following items for your graduation flight:

- A small bottle of water or juice for a dry mouth and perhaps a small bag of ice (no sodas with caffeine)

- Tissues for sweaty palms

- Nasal spray or decongestant if you are congested

- Headache remedy of choice

- Any medicines you are taking regularly (in case of a delay)

- A sweater or jacket in case the pilot turns the air-conditioning too low (summer and winter)

- A tape or CD player if you intend to dance to the turbulence

- Crossword puzzles or a magazine to entertain you if you get bored (it is quite possible)

- Chewing gum to help relieve tension in the ears (chewing gum causes you to swallow more)

- Lens rewetting solution if you wear contacts

- Your laminated flight plan (Appendix C)

- The sights, sounds, smells, and sensations of flight (Appendix A)

Summary

In preparing for your graduation flight, you must decide on the nature of your problem and assemble a flight plan that you can use to cope with your responses to fear. Being prepared also requires that you do some practice runs to the airport and some imaginary flights using self-guided, coping imageries. Without this preparation, the knowledge you have acquired is not likely to help you.

Finally, in order to overcome your fear of flying, you must fly! Choose your first flight carefully and put yourself in control of every aspect of it. Then be prepared to keep on flying.

10

After Your First Successful Flight

After you complete your first successful flight, by which I mean a flight that corresponds to your objectives, the fight has just begun. I've already suggested that once you start flying you need to continue flying regularly. One fearful flyer took this advice so seriously that the week after his first successful flight he flew from Boston to Dallas, Dallas to Miami, Miami to San Juan and back, and Miami to Boston. Is this necessary? Probably not, but he had regained his ability to fly once before and then lost it because he did not fly enough. He vowed he would never allow that to happen to him again.

In this chapter I will talk more about how often and how far you should be flying to maintain your gains and continue to advance in your battle with your fear. However, continuing to fly is only one of an extensive list of things you need to do to make sure that you accomplish your goal of flying without fear. Each of the areas you need to tackle as you continue your recovery will be addressed.

How Much Should You Fly?

I recommend that you fly within three months of your first successful flight. I developed this rule of thumb based on experience with, and feedback from, people who took successful graduation flights in our fearful flyer seminars. Specifically, this recommendation is for you if you board the graduation flight and meet or exceed your own expectations (goals). This recommendation also applies if you can state with a high level of confidence that, when you next fly, you are sure that you can board the plane and handle whatever comes. On the other hand, if you complete a successful flight and are not 100 percent certain that you can board a plane in the future, but feel that you probably can, I recommend that you fly immediately, perhaps within a week of your flight. Why? Because confidence erodes with the passage of time, and if you have done well, but have some doubts, you need to go to work immediately on your fear. This means flying again, and soon.

What if you fly within three months and things go well? What then? In order to maintain your confidence after your first two flights, fly at least once or twice a year, even if the flight is only for the purpose of keeping your fear grounded. If you are not doing well after your first two flights, it may be time to seek some professional help, unless you can identify what it is (the irrational thoughts) that makes you uncomfortable when you fly. If you can determine your problem, continue to work on it by getting accurate information and, of course, continue to fly. The techniques outlined in Chapter 7, particularly disputing irrational beliefs, should be helpful in ridding yourself of the remnants of your fear.

Working on Contributing Fears

Some of the problems that contribute to the fear of flying are more resistant than others. Turbulence leads the list of resistant problems, so do not be surprised or discouraged if your fear of turbulence persists for a bit longer than your other concerns. Many fearful flyers take several flights, spaced over several months, to get over their concerns about turbulence. If turbulence continues to be a concern after three or four flights, review the causes of turbulence (discussed in Chapter 6) and begin to try to predict its occurrence. For example, when you fly over a mountain range, you are almost certain to hit some bumpy air. Try to predict when this will occur rather than sitting in your seat in dread of turbulence. You can also predict that turbulence will occur on a hot day when you land in Phoenix and when your plane takes off or lands and there are white, puffy clouds in the sky.

When you get to the airport, look into the sky and make a prediction about turbulence. It may also help you to ask the pilot if turbulence is expected during the next portion of the flight. As you were told earlier, each flight plan has a turbulence index for each segment of the flight, so the pilot has some indication of what to expect. If you are told that some turbulence is expected when the plane takes off and will continue during the flight, combat any fear that arises with the mantra, "Turbulence is a comfort issue." Remember to keep moving with the turbulence. It is only "a whole lot of shakin' going on!"

Simple Phobias

Throughout this book acrophobia and claustrophobia have been addressed simultaneously with aviophobia because so many people who are afraid to fly have these problems. In some instances, people who are claustrophobic or acrophobic are also afraid that the airplane will crash (aviophobia), so they have multiple problems. If you are avoiding flying because of the contributory fears of closed spaces and heights, or you have one of these fears and are also afraid the airplane will crash, this is a good time to begin an ambitious, vigorous attack on these concerns. By doing so, you can totally or partially alleviate your fear of flying. Fortunately, these fears are relatively easy to treat.

Invivo Desensitization: Exposing Yourself to Your Fear

There are at least three approaches that have been used to treat simple phobias, which include both claustrophobia and acrophobia. These are *invivo desensitization, counter conditioning,* and *emotional flooding.* Of these three procedures, I prefer invivo desensitization, which involves actually exposing yourself to the feared situation, but exposing yourself in a controlled way.

Recently I helped a woman who was afraid of elevators and airplanes work on her fear of elevators and other closed spaces. I began by having her develop an exposure hierarchy, which is a ranking of fearful situations from least scary to most scary. What follows is the hierarchy she constructed:

1. Glass elevator in shopping mall that only goes up and down one story.

2. New elevators that go no more than five stories.

3. New elevators that go up or down more than five stories.

4. New elevators without telephones.

5. Old elevators that go only one or two stories.

6. Old elevators that "drop" before they go up. (By drop she meant that, as the control mechanism on the elevator releases before ascending, the elevator seems to sink or start down.)

7. Old elevators that go more than two stories and do not have telephones.

Once the hierarchy was developed, we developed a plan for her to "expose" herself to a series of elevators. But before she began riding elevators, we reviewed the relaxation techniques she had learned in order to cope with her fear of flying. (These techniques are the ones discussed in Chapter 4.) When riding elevators or entering other closed spaces, it was essential that she felt in control of her mental and physical reactions to her fear if the unthinkable happened—the elevator became stuck. Most importantly, she needed to control her breathing during elevator "rides" in order to keep calm.

After reviewing the exposure hierarchy, I asked her to ride elevators, beginning with the one-story glass elevator in the shopping mall, on her own. After mastering the shopping mall elevator, I urged her to take the next step, which was to ride a new elevator up five stories, get off, reboard the elevator, and ride it to the ground floor. This process was repeated until she felt a sense of mastery over new elevators. I then asked her to take subsequent steps when she felt ready to do so. If at any point in the process she felt unable to handle a problem that developed, I accompanied her on the elevator until she was confident that she could complete the task on her own. If, at any time during the process, she experienced a setback, which was defined as either avoiding an elevator that she felt she had mastered or feeling extremely panicky (a SUDS score of eight or higher) on an elevator that she had mastered, she went back to a less fearful step on the hierarchy and rebuilt her confidence level by riding "safer" elevators.

In a totally self-administered treatment, another woman eliminated her claustrophobia by following a program that I outlined. At the outset, not only would this woman not get on an elevator, she avoided all situations in which she was cramped or confined or thought this might occur. She now takes all types of elevators, including those in the tallest buildings in New York. She, and the other woman described here, were willing to confront their fear on a regular basis until they brought it under control. This type of courage is essential in this process, just as it is in getting over the fear of flying.

This invivo desensitization approach also works with acrophobia. I know because I used it to help myself deal with my own fear of heights.

I first realized that I was acrophobic when I attended a college basketball game and sat in a steep upper balcony overlooking the floor. I spent the entire night with my arm hooked over the back of my seat so I would not "fall," which was physically impossible. I also had a bit of a shock some years later when I took the glass elevator on the outside of the Fairmont Hotel in San Francisco. Because the hotel sits on one of the highest hills in San Francisco, the elevator is very quickly high above the city as it starts toward the top. I looked down once, pressed myself against the back wall of the elevator, and hoped the ride to the top would end quickly.

I overcame this fear by gradually exposing myself to higher and higher places, both in glass elevators and in open spaces, being careful not to go too far beyond my comfort level. I am still not totally comfortable looking down from a height of ten stories when I am in an open area, such as the top of a building. However, I will lean over the balcony and look down to the floor below in spite of my fear. Best of all, I love glass elevators and would recommend them to anyone who is not afraid of heights. If you are afraid of heights, I recommend that you begin to confront your fear so that you will be able to enjoy the beauty that comes with riding glass elevators inside many hotels, such as the Marriott in Manhattan, and those outside hotels, such as the Fairmont.

Your Exposure Hierarchy

If you have a simple phobia, develop your own exposure hierarchy in the spaces provided here:

1. _____

2. _____

3. _____

4. _____

5. _____

6. _____

7. _____

8. _____

9. _____

10. _____

Next, develop a timetable for confronting your fear. Move ahead as quickly as you can, but never move so fast that you overrun your confidence. The best way to determine whether you are ready to proceed is to use the SUDS scale introduced in Chapter 4. Ask yourself this question, "On a scale of one to ten, with one being no confidence and ten being complete confidence, how confident am I that I can handle the next step on my exposure hierarchy?" If your confidence rating is less than seven, I suggest you spend more time working on the current step. If you are afraid of elevators, as was the case with the woman described earlier, and your next step is a ride to the top of a very tall building and you are not confident that you can complete that step, spend more time taking short rides on elevators before you proceed. It is important that you also allow yourself to be spontaneous. If, for example, an opportunity presents itself to take the next step a bit earlier than you had planned, but you are 100 percent confident that you can go to the next step, do it. Admittedly, this is a bit of a risk, but your goal is to begin to trust yourself. It's no fun allowing your fear to control you.

You may reach a point in your exposure hierarchy where you seem to be stuck—that is, you cannot move to the next, more difficult step. If this happens, try inserting a "bridge." Your bridge may be to take the next step with a support person or hiring a therapist to help you get unstuck. Usually, however, it only means spending more time on the current step and practicing your relaxation skills. Controlling your physiological response to fear may give you the confidence you need to move ahead. The statement, "I'm scared, but I'm doing it," is often heard from people who are facing their fear. Some are ashamed of their fear and thus shamed by uttering this statement.

You'll Need Courage and Persistence

People who move ahead in the face of fear are truly courageous and should be patting themselves on the back. One of the pilots I worked with once told a seminar that he had witnessed more courage in the just-completed seminar than he had in all the battles he had fought in Vietnam. That's quite a statement about the courage of supposedly fearful people.

Another approach that helps some people who are having trouble moving up their exposure hierarchy is to spend so much time on the step at which they are stuck that they become bored doing it. The boredom with the current step, plus the desire to move ahead in the process of conquering your fear may just be the motivation you need to move to the next step.

Finally, never push yourself so hard that you avoid the task you have set for yourself. Avoidance is the primary mechanism in heightening your fear because of all the physical relief it gives you and because you believe you have escaped from a potentially dangerous situation. If you do avoid a task, lower your sights by going back to a step on your hierarchy that you are confident you can perform and rebuild your confidence. You will find that, by returning to a less threatening step on your hierarchy, you can rebuild your confidence in your ability to proceed rather easily.

Panic Attacks

The approaches to dealing with panic attacks are far too complicated to cover in a few paragraphs. Some self-directed approaches to dealing with panic attacks are described in references in Appendix B. I have known a few people who have rid themselves of panic attacks by using these references and others. However, if you are having panic attacks and have not consulted a good cognitive behavioral therapist (CBT), I suggest that you do so immediately, even if you are on medication that is helping. As you know by now, my philosophy is to use medication as an adjunct rather than the sole approach to therapy. A skilled CBT helped one of my daughters eliminate her panic attacks within a few months without medication. My daughter chose this approach, not out of opposition to medication, but because of her hypersensitivity to any type of medication and fear of side effects. Not surprisingly, she learned during the course of her therapy that her irrational, perfectionistic beliefs were at the core of her problem. Once she learned that being perfect is impossible for mortals, she began to turn the situation around. She has been free of panic attacks for three years, primarily because she learned to deal with her irrational thinking, and she learned to control her body.

Trust and Control

As I noted in Chapter 2, people who are afraid to fly often have control issues, which when examined carefully, are related to their inability to trust other people. There are two ways to deal with this problem. One of these is getting information from a credible source and using it to counter the faulty logic. If you believe that you are safer in your own car because you have control of the steering wheel, it is time to take a look at the illusion you have created for yourself. You must begin to counter your beliefs, because you have no control over other drivers. There is no comparison between the degree of control you can exert in your car and the controls placed on a flight.

If information and countering your fears with new information is not sufficient, I recommend that you take up the matter of your control issue with a therapist. The objective of this therapy should be to confront the faulty logic that precludes or limits your ability to trust others.

You and the Media

There will be airline disasters in the future. There will also be unfavorable stories about the industry. Because I want you to be an informed flyer who votes for safety with your ticket purchase, I urge that you get as much information as you can about the industry, and that you lobby your local and national representatives to improve airline safety.

I strongly recommend against watching or reading detailed reports of disasters, particularly those that are printed or shown the day or two after a disaster. These reports are filled with grisly details and a lot of speculation about the cause of the accident. Begin your review after the National Transportation Safety Board begins its investigation and starts to release authoritative reports to the media. When reading or watching these reports, try to distinguish between factual information and speculative information inserted by the reporter. You may even wish to get a follow-up report on the conclusions reached by the NTSB. You can obtain these reports by calling the NTSB in Washington, D.C., about a year after the accident. Again, pay attention to the recommendations that are made to improve safety and follow up to see whether the Federal Aviation Administration acts on those recommendations. What you will find is that steps are taken after almost every accident to improve the safety of the airline industry.

Summary

Flying can open up the world to you. Conquering your fear of flying will energize you and may set you on the road to dealing with other concerns. Always remember that overcoming your fear is a step-by-step process. If you have a setback, retrace your steps and go forward again.

Appendix A

Sights, Sounds, Smells, and Sensations of Flight

This appendix lists the outstanding sights, sounds, smells, and sensations you will experience on your flight, beginning with sitting at the jet bridge after you board and ending with the landing and return to the jet bridge at your destination. I recommend you make a copy of this and carry it with you on your flights. Use it both to review what occurs at each stage of the flight and to remind yourself, when the fear rises, that the sights and sounds you are experiencing are normal.

Sitting at the Jet Bridge

1. The swish of air entering the plane.

2. High-pitched whine of aircraft hydraulic pumps.

3. Clunk of cargo doors closing after baggage is loaded.

4. Blink of lights as auxiliary power unit is started.

5. Chimes: one chime when passengers call flight attendants; one chime five minutes prior to push back; chime is heard as seat belt sign is illuminated.

6. Condensation may be seen coming from vents on hot, muggy days.

Leaving the Jet Bridge

(Note: The plane may be pushed back or leave under its own power. The latter approach is called a power back.)

1. Announcement from cockpit, "Flight attendants, prepare for departure."

2. If push back, very quiet. If power back, very noisy as thrust of engines reversed.

3. Sound of air coming into cabin stops.

4. Lights blink as engines are started. May occur three or four times.

Taxi to Runway

1. High-pitched whine or groaning noise as devices on wings are extended for takeoff. May not occur on some planes.

2. Brakes squeak and grind when plane slows or stops.

3. Flight attendants deliver safety instructions and instructions to discontinue use of certain electronic devices.

4. Bumping (thump) sound is heard as tires pass over expansion joints in taxiway.

5. May smell jet fuel if plane is directly behind another plane.

6. Chimes: will probably hear two chimes from time to time as flight attendants communicate with each other about the service.

Takeoff Roll

1. Announcement from cockpit, "Flight attendants, please prepare for takeoff."

2. Chimes: a single chime will be heard.

3. Sounds of tires bumping over expansion joints and rough spots in the runway.

4. You will be pushed gently back into your seat as plane accelerates.

5. At lift off a thud will be heard as wheels extend to the end of their struts.

Climb

1. Thump-bump-thump is heard as landing gear is raised and locked into place.

2. Groaning sound or high-pitched whine will be heard as devices on wings are retracted. This will occur at least three times.

3. Pressure pushing you back in your seat increases because of the angle of the climb and because you are accelerating.

4. Several seconds after takeoff you will feel yourself rise in your seat, and your stomach will react as the captain lowers the nose of the aircraft and reduces power. Plane is still increasing speed even though the sound of the engine is reduced.

5. May experience level-offs and climbs at some airports. Noise and pressure on your body will change when these occur.

6. Chimes: one chime at 1,500 feet and another at 10,000 feet. Chime at 10,000 feet signals flight attendants that sterile cockpit period is over and they may call the crew or bring them food and beverages.

7. Increase in speed (wind noise may increase) at 10,000 feet. Speed increases from 280 miles an hour to cruise speed and then levels off.

Cruise

1. Plane levels off, engine noise lessens, and, if there is no turbulent air ahead, seat belt sign is turned off.

2. Chimes: one chime as seat belt sign is turned off.

3. Announcement from cockpit, "Ladies and gentlemen, I'm expecting a smooth ride today so I'm turning off the seat belt sign. However, when you are in your seats, we advise you to keep your seat belts fastened."

4. You may experience some climbs and descents during the flight. These will be accompanied by changes in engine noise and minor bodily sensations.

Decent

1. Engine noise will lessen and pilot will lower nose of plane.

2. Chimes: one chime when seat belt sign is turned on; one chime at 10,000 feet to signal start of sterile cockpit and another at 1,500 feet.

3. Landing lights turned on at 18,000 feet. May reflect off clouds in rainy weather when flying at night.

4. Intermediate level-offs will occur at some airports.

5. As approach to airport begins, groan or high-pitched whine will be heard as devices on the wings are extended. This will occur at least three times.

6. Announcement, "Flight attendants, please prepare for landing," is made a few minutes prior to landing.

7. Thump-bump-thump will be heard as landing gear is lowered.

8. Noise level increases as pilot prepares the plane for touchdown.

Landing and Taxi to Jet Bridge

1. Touchdown may be soft or firm depending on weather and other conditions.

2. Devices on wings will pop up at touchdown.

3. Engine noise increases as thrust of engines is reversed.

4. Brakes will squeak and grind as they are applied.

5. You are likely to move forward against your seat belt.

6. A groan or high-pitched whine will be heard as devices on wings are retracted.

7. Lights will flicker as the auxiliary power unit is started.

8. Announcement, "Flight attendants, please prepare for gate arrival," will be heard.

9. Announcement, "Ladies and gentlemen, please stay seated until the plane is parked safely at the gate," will be heard from the cockpit.

10. Chimes: a single chime will be heard when the seat belt sign is turned off. You can now deplane.

Appendix B

Additional Resources for Fearful Flyers

Books

Baboir, S., and C. Goldman 1990. *Overcoming Panic Attacks: Strategies to Free Yourself from the Anxiety Trap.* Minneapolis, MN: CompCare.

Bourne, E.J. 1990. *The Anxiety & Phobia Workbook.* Oakland, CA: New Harbinger.

Davis, M., R.A. Eshelman, and M. McKay 1988. *The Relaxation & Stress Reduction Workbook.* Oakland, CA: New Harbinger.

Jeffers, S. 1987. *Feel the Fear and Do It Anyway.* New York: Fawcett Columbine.

Markway, B. G., C.N. Carmin, C.A. Pollard, and T. Flynn 1992. *Dying of Embarrassment.* Oakland, CA: New Harbinger.

Sternstein, E., and T. Gold 1990. *From Takeoff to Landing: Everything You Wanted to Know About Airplanes but Had No One to Ask.* New York: Pocket Books.

Tapes

Fanning, P. 1991. *Applied Relaxation Training.* Oakland, CA: New Harbinger.

Fanning, P. 1987. *Progressive Relaxation and Breathing,* Item 1. Oakland, CA: New Harbinger.

McKay, M. 1993. *Time Out From Stress,* Volume One. Oakland, CA: New Harbinger.

Relaxation & Meditation with Music & Nature. Santa Monica, CA: Delta Music Inc.

Appendix C

My Flight Plan

When I Board the Plane

1. _____

2. _____

3. _____

4. _____

If the Fear Comes (Techniques to Use)

1. _____

2. _____

3. _____

4. _____

5. _____

Other Concerns and Actions

1. _____

2. _____

3. _____

Other New Harbinger Self-Help Titles

Flying Without Fear, $12.95
Kid Cooperation: How to Stop Yelling, Nagging & Pleading and Get Kids to Cooperate, $12.95
The Stop Smoking Workbook: Your Guide to Healthy Quitting, $17.95
Conquering Carpal Tunnel Syndrome and Other Repetitive Strain Injuries, $17.95
The Tao of Conversation, $12.95
Wellness at Work: Building Resilience for Job Stress, $14.95
What Your Doctor Can't Tell You About Cosmetic Surgery, $13.95
An End of Panic: Breakthrough Techniques for Overcoming Panic Disorder, $17.95
On the Clients Path: A Manual for the Practice of Solution-Focused Therapy, $39.95
Living Without Procrastination: How to Stop Postponing Your Life, $12.95
Goodbye Mother, Hello Woman: Reweaving the Daughter Mother Relationship, $14.95
Letting Go of Anger: The 10 Most Common Anger Styles and What to Do About Them, $12.95
Messages: The Communication Skills Workbook, Second Edition, $13.95
Coping With Chronic Fatigue Syndrome: Nine Things You Can Do, $12.95
The Anxiety & Phobia Workbook, Second Edition, $15.95
Thueson's Guide to Over-The Counter Drugs, $13.95
Natural Women's Health: A Guide to Healthy Living for Women of Any Age, $13.95
I'd Rather Be Married: Finding Your Future Spouse, $13.95
The Relaxation & Stress Reduction Workbook, Fourth Edition, $17.95
Living Without Depression & Manic Depression: A Workbook for Maintaining Mood Stability, $17.95
Belonging: A Guide to Overcoming Loneliness, $13.95
Coping With Schizophrenia: A Guide For Families, $13.95
Visualization for Change, Second Edition, $13.95
Postpartum Survival Guide, $13.95
Angry All The Time: An Emergency Guide to Anger Control, $12.95
Couple Skills: Making Your Relationship Work, $13.95
Handbook of Clinical Psychopharmacology for Therapists, $39.95
The Warrior's Journey Home: Healing Men, Healing the Planet, $13.95
Weight Loss Through Persistence, $13.95
Post-Traumatic Stress Disorder: A Complete Treatment Guide, $39.95
Stepfamily Realities: How to Overcome Difficulties and Have a Happy Family, $13.95
Leaving the Fold: A Guide for Former Fundamentalists and Others Leaving Their Religion, $13.95
Father-Son Healing: An Adult Son's Guide, $12.95
The Chemotherapy Survival Guide, $11.95
Your Family/Your Self: How to Analyze Your Family System, $12.95
Being a Man: A Guide to the New Masculinity, $12.95
The Deadly Diet, Second Edition: Recovering from Anorexia & Bulimia, $13.95
Last Touch: Preparing for a Parent's Death, $11.95
Consuming Passions: Help for Compulsive Shoppers, $11.95
Self-Esteem, Second Edition, $13.95
Depression & Anxiety Management: An audio tape for managing emotional problems, $11.95
I Can't Get Over It, A Handbook for Trauma Survivors, $13.95
Concerned Intervention, When Your Loved One Won't Quit Alcohol or Drugs, $11.95
Redefining Mr. Right, $11.95
Dying of Embarrassment: Help for Social Anxiety and Social Phobia, $12.95
The Depression Workbook: Living With Depression and Manic Depression, $14.95
Risk-Taking for Personal Growth: A Step-by-Step Workbook, $14.95
The Marriage Bed: Renewing Love, Friendship, Trust, and Romance, $11.95
Focal Group Psychotherapy: For Mental Health Professionals, $44.95
Hot Water Therapy: Save Your Back, Neck & Shoulders in 10 Minutes a Day $11.95
Prisoners of Belief: Exposing & Changing Beliefs that Control Your Life, $10.95
Be Sick Well: A Healthy Approach to Chronic Illness, $11.95
Men & Grief: A Guide for Men Surviving the Death of a Loved One., $12.95
When the Bough Breaks: A Helping Guide for Parents of Sexually Abused Childern, $11.95
Love Addiction: A Guide to Emotional Independence, $12.95
When Once Is Not Enough: Help for Obsessive Compulsives, $13.95
The New Three Minute Meditator, $12.95
Getting to Sleep, $12.95
Beyond Grief: A Guide for Recovering from the Death of a Loved One, $13.95
Thoughts & Feelings: The Art of Cognitive Stress Intervention, $13.95
Leader's Guide to the Relaxation & Stress Reduction Workbook, Fourth Edition, $19.95
The Divorce Book, $11.95
Hypnosis for Change: A Manual of Proven Techniques, 2nd Edition, $13.95
The Chronic Pain Control Workbook, $14.95
When Anger Hurts, $13.95
Free of the Shadows: Recovering from Sexual Violence, $12.95
Lifetime Weight Control, $11.95
Love and Renewal: A Couple's Guide to Commitment, $13.95

Call **toll free, 1-800-748-6273**, to order. Have your Visa or Mastercard number ready. Or send a check for the titles you want to New Harbinger Publications, Inc., 5674 Shattuck Avenue, Oakland, CA 94609. Include $3.80 for the first book and 75¢ for each additional book, to cover shipping and handling. (California residents please include appropriate sales tax.) Allow four to six weeks for delivery.

Prices subject to change without notice.